# Descriptor Generation Techniques Based on Hierarchical-Scale and Multi-Orientation Transforms for Analyzing Form and Layout Characteristics in Aerial Data Classification

Enleveur Pecados

**Descriptor Generation Techniques Based on Hierarchical-Scale and Multi-Orientation Transforms for Analyzing Form and Layout Characteristics in Aerial Data Classification**

**First Edition June 2025**



**Written by Enleveur Pecados**

# TABLE OF CONTENTS

**CHAPTER NO.** **TITLE** **PAGE NO.**

## LIST OF TABLES

# LIST OF FIGURES

# LIST OF ABBREVIATIONS

| | | |
|---|---|---|
| AS | - | Accuracy Assessment |
| BCFCM | - | Bias Corrected Fuzzy C Means |
| CL | - | Chui-Lian |
| CI | - | Classified Image |
| CFT | - | Contourlet Frame Transform |
| DB2 | - | Daubachies Wavelet Filter 2 |
| DEM | - | Digital Elevation Model |
| DTM | - | Digital Terrain Model |
| DFB | - | Directional Filter Banks |
| ERS | - | European Remote Sensing |
| FR | - | Feature Reduction |
| FVF | - | Feature Vector Formation |
| Ft | - | Feet |
| FT | - | Fourier Transform |
| FCM | - | Fuzzy C Means |
| GKFCM | - | Gaussian Kernel Fuzzy C Means |
| GIS | - | Geographical Information Systems |
| GHM | - | Geronimo, Hardin and Massopust |
| GLCM | - | Gray Level Co occurance Matrix |
| GCP | - | Ground Control Points |
| H | - | Highpass |
| IRS | - | Indian Remote Satellite |
| ISRO | - | Indian Space Research Organization |
| HIS | - | Intensity Hue Saturation |
| K | - | Kappa |

| | |
|---|---|
| KFCM | - Kernel Fuzzy C Means |
| KPCA | - Kernel Principal Component Analysis |
| Km | - Kilometer |
| LDA | - Linear Discriminant Analysis |
| LISS | - Linear Imaging Self Scanner |
| L | - Low Pass |
| M | - Meter |
| MSMR | - Microfrequency Scanning Microwave Radiometer |
| Mid IR | - Mid Infra red |
| MCT | - MultiContourlet Transform |
| Mx | - Multispectral mode |
| MWFT | - Multiwavelet Frame Transform |
| MWT | - Multiwavelet transform |
| NRSC | - National Remote Sensing Centre |
| NIR | - Near Infra red |
| NSDFB | - Non Subsampled Directional Filter Banks |
| NSPFB | - Non Subsampled Pyramidal filter Banks |
| NSCT | - Nonsubsampled Contourlet transform |
| NDVI | - Normalized Difference Vegetation Index |
| NE | - North East |
| NW | - North West |
| NDC | - NRSC Data Centre |
| OCM | - Ocean Colour Monitor |
| PAN | - Panchromatic |
| PVI | - Perpendicular Vegetation index |
| PSLV | - Polar Satellite Launch Vehicle |
| PR | - Practical Pattern Recognition Problem |
| PCA | - Principal Component Analysis |

| | | |
|---|---|---|
| ROSA | - | Radio occultation sound for atmoshphere |
| SDSC | - | Satish Dhawan Space Centre |
| OSCAT | - | Scatterometer |
| SE | - | South East |
| SW | - | South West |
| CNES | - | Space Agency of France |
| SWT | - | Stationary Wavelet Transform |
| SVM | - | Support Vector Machine |
| SAR | - | Synthetic Aperture Radar |
| 3D | - | Three Dimension |
| TOA | - | Top of Atmoshphere Reflectance |
| 2D | - | Two Dimension |
| WBCT | - | Wavelet Based Contourlet Transform |
| WFT | - | Wavelet Frame Transform |
| WT | - | Wavelet Transform |
| WIFS | - | Wide Field Sensor |

# CHAPTER 1

# INTRODUCTION

This chapter provides an overview of remote sensing stages, optical remote sensing, multispectral imaging system, applications and challenges of remote sensing and the list of Indian remote sensing satellites. In the literature review section, details about the Indian satellite image analysis, LISS II, LISS III, LISS IV image analysis, multi resolution and multi scale texture feature extraction, feature reduction and feature classification. This chapter also provides research objectives, contribution and organization of the thesis.

## 1.1 OVERVIEW

Remote sensing is a process used for gathering information about an object or phenomenon without making physical contact with the object and it refers to the activities of recording/observing/ perceiving (sensing) objects or events at far away (remote) places. The remote sensing satellites are equipped with sensors looking down to the earth. They are known as the "eyes in the sky". They constantly observe the earth as they go round in predictable orbits and were used to detect and classify objects in the earth by means of propagated signals (e.g. electromagnetic radiation). Remote sensing data utilizes the electromagnetic radiation that is reflected or emitted from the surface of an object. The process of remote sensing is shown in Figure.1.1.

Remote sensors for example cameras or scanners mounted on satellites or aircraft collect data by energy that is reflected from the earth. They are of two types, 1) active, 2) passive. Passive sensors utilize reflected sunlight as a source of radiation and gathers natural radiation that is emitted or reflected by the object or the surrounding areas. On the contrary, active sensors can generate and detect their own source of energy and are used in the region.

In remote sensing the satellite sensors, that are not in direct contact with the object are observed. The electromagnetic radiation act as physical career carrying information from the objects / events to sensors through an intervening medium.

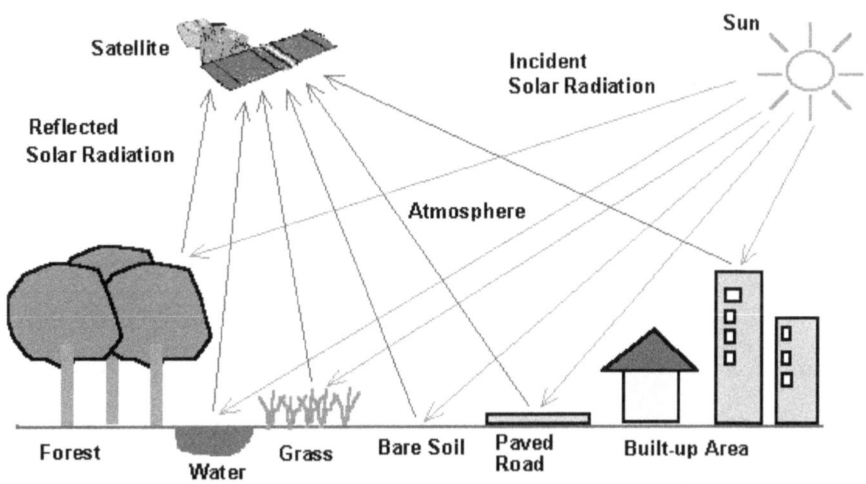


(Source - http://www.crisp.nus.edu.sg/~research/tutorial/intro.htm)

**Figure 1.1 Process of remote sensing**

Usually the output of the remote sensing is an image that represents the scene being observed. Later the output image should be analyzed, interpreted to extract useful information from the image.

### 1.1.1 Remote Sensing Stages

The remote sensing process involves two stages:

- Data collection and
- Data analysis

Data collection is accomplished through the use of remote sensing devices that record data on the photographic film or digital data. The resulting data provides a synoptic view of a portion of the earth"s surface, but requires analysis and interpretation in order to provide meaningful information. Thus involve visual interpretation which has been the predominant mode of air photo interpretation or digital analysis, which has been widely used in processing satellite imagery. With the aid of the reference data, the analyst extracts the information about the location, type, extent and condition of the various resources over which the sensor data were collected. This information is then compiled, generally in the form of hardcopy maps and tables or as the computer files that can be merged with other layers of information in geographic information systems. Finally, the end users will use the derived information in the decision making process. The main benefits provided by remotely sensed data are,

- The ability to update research with new data multiple times per year.
- The ability to obtain information about areas of the earth that would otherwise be very difficult to reach, physically and/or financially.

### 1.1.2 Optical Remote Sensing

Optical remote sensors are those that detect solar radiation in visible, near infrared and thermal-infrared wavelength regions that are reflected/scattered or emitted from the earth. Most of the remote sensing systems record energy over multiple wavelengths at different spectral resolutions and hence referred as multi-spectral sensors. Land features like water, soil, vegetation, cloud and snow were capable of reflecting visible and infrared light in different ways. The way of explaining the optical images requires the technical knowledge of spectral reflectance patterns of various natural and artificial materials covering the surface of the earth.

Different visual elements of interpretation like shape, size, tone or hue, texture, pattern, shadow, location/ association were used to interpret the images. Depending upon the number of spectral bands employed in imaging process, the optical remote sensing system was classified into four types,

- Panchromatic Imaging System
- Multispectral Imaging System
- Superspectral Imaging System
- Hyperspectral Imaging System

### 1.1.3 Multispectral Imaging System

The multispectral image consists of several bands of data. During visual display, these bands are displayed as one band at a time as a gray scale image or as a combination of three to seven bands at a time as colour composite image. To interpret the multispectral colour composite image, idea on the spectral reflectance signatures of the targeted area is mandatory. For the interpretation of the digital image, spectral information content of the image is utilized.

### 1.1.4 Applications & Challenges of Remote Sensing

Remote sensing generated satellite images that in turn derive a wide range of information which are widely utilized in variety of applications like land use, land cover changes, urban sprawl identification, temporal changes between the terrain conditions, forest and agriculture status assessment, drought monitoring etc. Table 1.1 shows the applications of remote sensing in different areas. The output of the remote sensing arrives in the form of a digital image which enables the end users to extract useful information from the digital image in a rapid and efficient manner. Several remote sensors at present on earth orbiting satellite platforms provides at the different level of digital images, and satellite image processing is an important tool to exploit this resource.

**Table 1.1 Applications of remote sensing**

| Agriculture & Soil | Rural & urban |
|---|---|
| • Crop Production<br>• Irrigation<br>• Cropping Pattern<br>• Crop Yield<br>• Soil | • Rural<br>• Urban<br>• Cadastral<br>• Policy<br>• International Experience |
| Archaeology | Utility |
| • General<br>• Site Prediction<br>• Database Management | • Telecommunications<br>• Power<br>• Transport<br>• Water |

<table>
<tr><td>Biodiversity – Ecology<ul><li>Conservation and Planning</li><li>Wildlife Management</li><li>Wetland Ecosystem</li></ul></td><td>Health<ul><li>Overview</li><li>Planning and Monitoring</li></ul></td></tr>
<tr><td>Environment<ul><li>Policy</li><li>Planning</li><li>Monitoring and Management</li></ul></td><td>Urban Planning<ul><li>Urban Sprawl</li><li>Fringe Area Development</li><li>Urban Agglomeration</li><li>Cultural Resource Management</li></ul></td></tr>
<tr><td>Geology<ul><li>Mineral and Mining</li><li>Neotectonics</li><li>Geological Mapping</li><li>Engineering Geology</li></ul></td><td>Military<ul><li>Image Resolution</li><li>Intrusion detection</li><li>Navigation</li></ul></td></tr>
<tr><td>Geomorphology<ul><li>Fluvial</li><li>Glacial</li><li>Eolian</li><li>Morphometric Analysis</li><li>Slopes</li></ul></td><td>Natural Hazards<ul><li>Earthquakes</li><li>Floods</li><li>Cyclone/Storms</li><li>Drought</li><li>Fire</li><li>Volcano Hazards</li><li>Disaster Monitoring</li><li>Landslides/Soil Erosion</li></ul></td></tr>
</table>

Challenges of Remote Sensing

There are many challenges involved in terrestrial remote sensing. Only 4% of the incoming solar radiation is reflected back off the Earth's surface and a further 5% is re-radiated after absorption as thermal energy. Nevertheless, it is these two components that are the focus of most terrestrial remote sensing.

Only selected wavelengths are able to penetrate the earth's atmosphere and be reflected back to an airborne or space borne sensor. Thus only some wavelengths are available for analysis and some objects of interest may not have unique spectral signatures within the set of available wavelengths.

Furthermore, reflected radiation may be attenuated by the atmosphere due to haze or clouds. Thus the signal reaching the sensor may include reflection off the Earth's surface that contains information about features and conditions on the surface, but it also includes in-coming and reflected EMR that has been scattered by the atmosphere. This can result in a loss of details in the resulting images, making interpretation more difficult.

### 1.1.5 Importance of Land Use / Land Cover Mapping

Under the current world situation, land use and land cover mapping plays a vital role in scientific, scholarly research, planning and management. Regional land use pattern explains the pattern of interaction between the man and environment and the effect of distance and the resources based on mankind"s basic economic activities. Remote sensing satellites provides a bird"s eye view of the entire study area in a short period of time that results in rapid and reliable representation of the real world. These mapping effectively establishes the co-ordination between the industrial, transportation, residential and recreational land uses, besides providing broad-scale inventories of natural resources and monitoring various environmental issues, including land reclamation, mangrove restoration, disaster relief, water quality and planning economic development.

Land use cover features have been precisely captured through on screen visual interpretation and digitally fused on very high resolution ranging from 0.60 m, Quick Bird and medium to coarse resolution (LISS II, LISS III, LISS IV) satellite imagery. Such maps will provide a clarity view of the total area thereby helping the town planners to plan an efficient and best possible utilization of its resources.

### 1.1.6 List of Indian Remote Sensing Satellites

The remote sensing satellites aimed to provide necessary continuity of operational services in an assured manner in relatively wide area like land and water resources management, the cartographic and large scale mapping applications, and the ocean and atmospheric research areas. The different Indian Remote Sensing Satellites are shown in Table 1.2. National Remote Sensing Centre (NRSC) is the nodal point for distribution of remote sensing satellite data products in India and its neighbouring countries. The ground earth station of NRSC was at Shadnagar which was about 5 km from Hyderabad.

**Table 1.2 List of Indian remote sensing satellites**

| Satellite Name | Year | Spatial Resolution(Meter) | Altitute(Km) |
|---|---|---|---|
| IRS 1A | 1988 | 36.25 Mx | 893/913 |
| IRS 1B | 1991 | 36.25 Mx | 890/917 |
| IRS 1C | 1995 | 23.6 Mx | 816/818 |
| IRS P3 | 1996 | 189 WiFS | 802/848 |
| IRS 1D | 1997 | 23 Mx<br>6 PAN<br>189 WIFS | 736/825 |
| IRS P4-OCEANSAT | 1999 | 360× 236 | 720 |
| IRS P6 – RESOURCESAT | 2003 | 5.8 Mx & PAN | 821 |
| CARTOSAT-1 | 2005 | 2,5 PAN | 618 |
| CARTOSAT -2 | 2007 | Less than 1 m | 630 |
| CARTOSAT-2A | 2008 | Less than 1 m | 637 |
| OCEANSAT-2 | 2009 | 50,000 | 720 |
| CARTOSAT -2B | 2010 | 1 | 630 |
| RESOURCESAT-2 | 2011 | 5.8 | 817 |
| MEGHA-TROPIQUES | 2011 | 40,000 | 865 |
| RISAT-1 SAR | 2012 | 1 | 480 |

The major mandate of this station was to collect data from all neighbouring remote sensing satellites. The NDC possess a range of data products with a wide choice of media and formats. The first event Indian Space Programme began with the launch of India‟s first civilian remote sensing satellite IRS-1A in March 1988. IRS-1A was the first remote sensing satellite undertaken by Indian Space Research Organization to provide imageries for various land use land cover applications. This satellite carries two sensors 'Linear Imaging Self-Scanning System' cameras, LISS-I and LISS-II, with a spatial resolution of 72.5 metres (238 ft) and 36.25 m respectively. **IRS-1A** has successfully completed its life time in July 1996. The operating time for the satellite was 8 years and 4 months.

**IRS-1B** has successfully completed its life time 4 months in December 2003. The operating time for the satellite is 12 years 4 months.

**IRS.-1C** was the fourth remote sensing Indian satellite launched by Indian Space Research Organization. The primary use of IRS-1C was to provide systematic and repetitive acquisition of data of the Earth"s surface under nearly constant illumination conditions.

**IRS-1D** was the seventh satellite launched by Indian Remote Sensing satellite series of Earth. The satellite carries the instruments onboard panchromatic camera with spatial resolution of 5.8 m, Linear Imaging Self Scanner with spatial resolution of 23.5 m, Wide Field Sensor (WIFS) with a ground resolution of 188 m.

**IRS P6/Resourcesat-1 and Resourcesat-2** ensures the continuity of medium and high resolution data supply provided by the twin satellites IRS-1C and IRS-1D. Resourcesat satellites carry the LISS-IV sensor which is a high resolution (5.8 m) multi-spectral camera operating in green, red and near infrared spectral bands. The high-resolution data are useful for applications such as urban planning and mapping, while the average resolution is used for vegetation discrimination, land mapping and natural resources management.

LISS-IV can be operated in either of the two modes. In the multi-spectral mode (Mx), a swath of 23.5 Km is covered in three bands, while in mono mode (Mono), the full swath of 70 Km can be covered in any one single band selectable by ground command.

**CARTOSAT – 1** was launched on May 5, 2005 on board PSLV - C6 from Satish Dhawan Space Centre (SDSC), Sriharikota. The satellite possess two panchromatic cameras viz., PAN (fore) and PAN (aft) with a resolution and swath of 2.5 m and 30km, respectively. The data generated from CARTOSAT-1 satellite is used for the construction of cartographic maps, updation of cadastral maps, various land use and GIS applications. It has also an onboard solid state recorder that provides information about the ground area that invisible. The two cameras were usually mounted at a tilt of +/1 26 degree and -5 degree along the track with respect to the nadir that yields stereo pairs of images which were in turn utilized to generate Digital Terrain Model (DTM) / Digital Elevation Model (DEM).

**CARTOSAT – 2** is an advanced version of remote sensing satellite and stands twelfth in the Indian Remote Sensing (IRS) satellite series that provides scene-specific spot imagery. It was launched on January 10, 2007 and carries a single panchromatic camera onboard capable of providing better than 1-metre spatial resolution imagery, with a swath of 9.6 km. The satellite can be steered up to +/-45 degree along and +/- 26 deg across the track to facilitate imaging of any area more frequently.

**OCEANSAT-1** is a satellite launched by onboard PSLV - C2 in May 1999 with specified application to study the physical and biological features of oceanography that carries Ocean Colour Monitor (OCM) and a Multifrequency Scanning Microwave Radiometer (MSMR). Ocean Colour Monitor operates in a frequency of 402-422, 433-453, 480-500, 500-520, 545-565, 660-689, 745-785 and 845-885 nm bands with 360 meter spatial resolution and 1420 km swath. The monitor gathers information over the Indian region operationally.

**OCEANSAT- 2** is a satellite craft of ISRO that was designed to provide service to the users of ocean data and to increase the potential in other areas like studies related to surface winds, ocean surface strata, data on concentration of chlorophyll in leaves, monitoring of phytoplankton blooms, study of atmospheric aerosols and suspended sediments in the water. The satellite OCEANSAT – 2 contains the three payloads viz., Ocean Colour Monitor (OCM), Ku-band Pencil Beam scatterometer (OSCAT) and Radio Occultation Sounder for Atmosphere (ROSA).

**RESOURCESAT – 1** stands tenth in the hierarchy of IRS and was launched on board PSLV - C5 in October 2003. It was launched at Synchronous Orbit at a height of 820km with three cameras.

**RESOURCESAT -2** is the improved version of RESOURCESAT -1 and is the eighteenth remote sensing satellite built by ISRO. The data services provided by RESOURCESAT – 2 were similar to that provided by RESOURCESAT – 1 but with better or improved multispectral and spatial coverage.

**RISAT – 1** is the first satellite imaging mission of ISRO that uses C - band imager with a Synthetic Aperture Radar (SAR). The satellite use day and night SAR observation and weather data to generate valuable information in agriculture, forestry, soil moisture, geology, sea ice, coastal monitoring, object identification and flood monitoring.

**RISAT – 2** is a Synthetic Aperture Radar (SAR) is the first satellite imagery that was launched with by Indian PSLV - CA launch vehicle and is used to monitor all weather related parameters day to night thereby aids in disaster management effectively.

**MEGHA-TROHIQUES** is an Indo French joint satellite that provides scientific data on the role of water cycle in tropical atmosphere. In addition to this, it collects data on condensed water on clouds, water vapour in atmosphere, rain and evaporation. Ultimately the objective of the mission is to gain knowledge about the heating systems that affect the weather and moisture conditions of the tropical belts. This satellite mission targets a circular orbit at an angle of 20 degrees inclined with respect to equator and therefore serves as a viable tool for the climate research. The satellite aids the scientists to rebuild the prediction models.

**SARAL** or Satellite with ARgos and ALtiKa is a joint altimetry technology and is a joint venture of ISRO (Indian Space Research Organization) and CNES (Space Agency of France). The objectives were to clear repeated global measurements of sea surface height, significant wave heights and wind speed to develop operational oceanography, study of mesoscale ocean viability, coastal region observations, sea water ecosystems and inland waters and to understand the weather forecasting and operational meteorology.

## 1.2 LITERATURE REVIEW

### 1.2.1 Literature on Indian Satellite Image Analysis

Research using images captured by Indian Remote Sensing Satellites are also found in literature. (Negi et al. 2012) Gangotri glacier area was monitored using Indian Remote Sensing (IRS) LISS-III sensor data in addition with field collected snow-meteorological data over a period of seven years (2001–2008).The study revealed an overall decrease in the aerial extent of seasonal snow cover area.

Subudhi et al. (1989) analyzed IRS LISS II data corresponding to Delhi metropolitan area to demonstrate its potentiality in urban applications in which various image processing algorithms were discussed to show the suitability for urban area studies.

Mattia & Laura (2009) proposed a procedure to evaluate the various image quality parameters. These procedures was implemented in suitable software and tested on high resolution imagery acquired by the Quick Bird, WorldView-1 and Cartosat-1 satellites.

Amitabh et al. (2009) reported about the methodology to generate and update a 1:25000 topographical map using Cartosat-1 and Cartosat-2 images in an integrated approach. The process included data pre-processing, DEM and Ortho-image generation, modelling of space imagery, accuracy improvement of DEM and Ortho-image, Image to Image registration, 2D and 3D feature extraction and mapping in a standard cartographic environment.

Kimothi et al. (2010) examined the utility of Indian remote sensing satellite data for the detection and mapping of the patch information extraction of the invasive weed, lantana camera. IRS LISS IV and LISS IV with Cartosat-1 merged data were used to test their suitability. The merged product facilitated maximum differentiation (96.4%) followed by LISS IV (92.9%).

Raju (2013) reported that megha tropiques is an Indo-French satellite mission built using ISRO"s IRS platform and four high technology payloads meant for climate research and applications in tropical regions.

### 1.2.2 Literature on LISS II, LISS III, LISS IV Image Analysis

Research using images captured by Indian Remote Sensing Satellites LISS II, LISS III, LISS IV are found in literature. Babu (2012) conducted a spectral analysis on the IRS P6 LISS III images to identify the gold associated minerals in Veligallu Schist Belt, Kadapa district, (Ghosh et al 2000) described the mapping of tea gardens from Indian Remote Sensing Satellite Linear Imaging Self Scanner II geocoded images of an area in the district of Cacher in Assam, India has been carried out for mapping of tea gardens in cacher district in Assam ,India

Rahman et al. (2004) used normalized difference vegetation index in IRS LISS II digital data for identifying the sugarcane area and its crop condition assessment. (Dinesh 1998) proposed a fuzzy multistage ISODATA algorithm for the classification of remotely sensed data for the IRS 1B LISS-II image of Nagarhole forest in India.

Hebbara & Sai (2014) carried out a study for selection of suitable LISS-IV Mx band for data fusion and its evaluation for delineation different crops in a multi-cropped area in East Godavari district of Andhra Pradesh, India. For the selection of suitable LISS-IV Mx band for data fusion and its evaluation for delineation different crops in a multi-cropped area in East Godavari district of Andhra Pradesh, India, the fusion operation was performed on the IRS 1D images combined with LISS III data and ERS radar data. The results of classification accuracy were compared and the best results was obtained by combining IRS ID image data by means of IHS colour transformation technique and the results suggested that combining IRS 1D image with LISS III data gave better accuracy results.

Kaliraj & Chandrasekar (2012) applied spectral recognition techniques and Maximum likelihood classifiers on the IRS P6 LISS III images to extract the coastal landforms in the south west coast of Tamil Nadu India. Dwivedi& Ramana (2001) compare the merging of high spatial resolution panchromatic data having resolution 5.8m with IRS LISS II and LISS III data. Over all accuracy of LISS II, LISS III, PAN with the IHS transformation on the order of 89.6 percent, 85.9 percent, 81.5 percent respectively.

Javed et al. (2012) identified and quantified climate change induced land degradation at watershed village level in jaggar watershed of eastern Rajasthan. This study utilized LISS II data of 1989, LISS III data of 1998 and 2009 for land use land cover mapping.

Zhang & Tian (2015) compared the NIR band of LISS III with the two NIR bands of ALI the result showed that the distinct linear correlation exists between the spectral characteristics of LISS III and ALI, the correlation value ranged between 0.976 to 0.995 and the TOA reflectance from 0.992 to 0.997

Hoseini & Darvishsefat (2012) investigated the capability of IRS-P6-LISS IV satellite image for pistachio forests density mapping in northeast of Iran. Suitable spectral transformations like NDVI, PVI and PCA were performed. The highest overall accuracy and kappa coefficient of 70% and 0.44, respectively, were obtained with three classes (0-5%, 5-20%, and >20%) by fuzzy classifier.

Gupta & Jain (2005) evaluated the information content available in IRS P6 LISS IV data and PAN sharpened LISS III data for the identification of urban features and urban mapping in Dehradun city. It was found that 100

% more linear features could be extracted with IRS P6 LISS IV compared to PAN sharpened LISS III data.

Kiran & Srivastava (2015) conducted a case study in Simlipal Block, Bankura District, West Bengal for Infrastructure Updation and Land Use/Land Cover Mapping. (Radhadevi et al 2009) described a method for co-registration of multiple bands of LISS-IV camera through photogrammetric means using the collinearity equations.

### 1.2.3 Literature on Texture Analysis

Image classification is a vital process in many image vision applications, which involves partitioning an input image into different isolated regions, such that each region represents common properties and represents a different object. Texture analysis offers interesting possibilities to characterize the heterogeneity of classes. Texture features play an important role in motion detection (Dumontier et al 1999),video surveillance (Collins et al 2000) & medical images (Abu-Zeid et al 2012).The texture of an image is related to the spatial distribution of the intensity values in the image, and as such contains information regarding contrast, uniformity, rigidity, regularity, etc. In texture analysis, the most important task is to extract texture features which efficiently represent the textural characteristics of the original image. These features can then be used for description or classification of different texture images. A large collection of literature on image classification based on textures has been proposed over the past decades. These algorithms may be based on spectral, statistical, geometrical or structural, model based or signal processing methods

Weszka et al. (1976) reported the relatively poor performance of Fourier power spectrum, second-order gray level statistics and on first order statistics of gray level differences in the classification of terrain samples. Haralick (1979) reported that structural statistical generalizations that will apply for the statistical techniques to structural primitives. Various statistical approaches like auto correlation function, optical transforms, digital transforms, texture edgeness, structure element, gray tone co-occurrence, autoregressive models and run lengths were used.

Robert et al. (1973) reported the utility of easily computable features based on spatial gray level dependencies and their application in category identification and image processing applications from the three different kinds of data namely photo micro graphs, aerial photographs and multispectral imagery.

Unser & Eden (1988) reported that Karhunen - Loeve transform feature reduction measure was improved using local linear transforms that have been optimized for maximal texture discrimination for extraction of local texture properties.

Randen et al. (1999) reported about the major filtering methods for texture feature extraction like Laws masks, ring and wedge filters, dyadic Gabor filter banks, wavelet transforms, wavelet packets and wavelet frames, quadrature mirror filters, discrete cosine transform, eigen filters, optimized Gabor filters, linear predictors, and optimized finite impulse response filters. These features were considered as the local energy of filter responses in which effect of the filtering is highlighted, whereas the local energy function and the classification algorithm was considered the same for most of the approaches.

Singh & Singh (2002) reported few traditional techniques of texture analysis like MeasTex and VisTex benchmarks to illustrate their relative abilities. This technique includes autocorrelation function, co-occurrence matrices, edge frequency, Law"s masks, run length, binary stack method, texture operators, and texture spectrum. The advantage of using feature selection on a combined set to improve the overall recognition performance was illustrated. Based on these literature reviews statistical based texture feature extraction requires more computational time to calculate the feature matrix. The accuracy of the statistical frame based features gave less accuracy.

### 1.2.4 Literature on Multi Resolution & Multi Scale based Texture Feature Extraction

Many researchers have dealt with the non- stationary behaviour of signals using Fourier transform. The Fourier Transform (FT) method assumes a stationary signal within its total range of analysis. To overcome this disadvantage, the Wavelet Transform (WT) was used that does not lose the spatial localization of the signal frequencies.

Unser (1995) reported about the characterization of texture properties at multiple scales using the wavelet transform which uses a complete wavelet decomposition that yields a description that is translation invariant. The results suggested the superior performance of wavelet transform over most traditional single resolution techniques.

Acharyya & Kundu (2001) reported a texture feature extraction based on M-Band wavelet frames. Discrete M-Band wavelet packet transform is an over complete wavelet decomposition scheme gives the improved segmentation results unlike dyadic wavelets. Wavelet packets represent the generalization of the method of multi resolution decomposition and comprise all possible combinations of sub band tree decomposition.

Acharyya & Kundu (2001a) discussed about the texture feature extraction based on M-Band wavelet decomposition. M band wavelet packet frame consists of an over complete wavelet decomposition scheme that yields improved segmentation accuracies in which most of the significant information lies in the intermediate frequency bands of input images. In this method, a computationally efficient search procedure was used to find the optimal basis based on some maximum criterion of textural measures derived from the statistical parameters of each of the sub bands, to locate dominant information in each frequency channels and further decomposition was decided.

Acharyya et al. (2003) suggested unsupervised classification technique using M Band wavelet packet frames in which neuro fuzzy algorithm was used to evaluate the features. The accuracy of the methodology was tested on two four band Indian remote sensing satellite (IRS-1A) images consists of six overlapping classes and a three band spot image consisted of seven overlapping classes.

Arivazhagan & Ganeshan (2003) reported the texture classification using four methods *viz.,* i) wavelet statistical based features, (ii) wavelet co-occurrence based features and (iii) a combination of different wavelet statistical features and co-occurrence features of one level wavelet transformed images with different feature databases. Among the three methods, the combination of wavelet statistical and co occurrence features gave better promising results.

Arivazhagan et al. (2006) discussed Gabor wavelet based rotation invariant features for texture classification. Wavelet transform lacked its ability to decompose the input image in to multiple orientations. On the contrary, Gabor wavelet divided the input images in to multiple scales and multiple orientations.

Meher et al. (2007) reported the multispectral features are extracted using wavelets from remote sensing images for land cover classification. Wavelet provides spatial and spectral characteristics of a pixel along with its neighbours and hence this can be used for improved classification. Four classifiers namely fuzzy product aggregation reasoning rule (FPARR), fuzzy explicit, multilayer perceptron and Neuro Fuzzy were used. Biorthogonal 3.3 frame based features with Fuzzy product aggregation reasoning rule gave better accuracy results compared to four classifiers.

Alaguraja et al. (2009) discussed the application of wavelet frame based texture classification technique was applied to the Madurai city multispectral images. Lemaire Battle wavelet frame was used to extract the features and is inputted to the fuzzy c means classifier in which four indices producer, user, overall and kappa were used to measure the accuracy. The results showed the superior accuracy results of Lemaire battle wavelet frame based features compared to statistical frame based feature extraction techniques.

Kavitha et al. (2010) reported the importance of feature extraction and classifier selection for the improvement of classification accuracy. Wavelet based textural feature extraction was entailed. Hyper spectral images have dozen numbers of bands in which few bands are selected and wavelet transform was applied. For each sub band, GLCM values are calculated. From GLCMs co-occurrence features were derived for individual pixels. In addition to co-occurrence features, statistical features were also calculated.

Rajesh et al. (2012) analyzed the performance of a combination of Wavelet Packet Statistical Features and Wavelet Packet Co-occurrence features for the classification of Linear Imaging Self Scanner (LISS) IV images in which the classification accuracy per pixel was improved by varying the window size. The results suggested that multiband and multilevel wavelet packet approach can be used to drastically increase the classification accuracy. Accuracy indices indicated that Daubechies wavelet filter (DB2) yielded superior results compared to the other wavelet filters thereby more useful for Land cover/Land use mapping. From the literature review wavelet based features gives multi resolution features and fails to give directional features. Most of the features lies in the intermediate frequency -bands. For directional selectivity an efficient transform was needed.

Alaguraja et al. (2013) reported the utility of wavelet frame based post classification change detection technique is applied to identify the urban changes and to find newly fringe urban area between the Madurai city during 1996 and 2004. In this method, Coiflet wavelet was used to derive the features and given for fuzzy classification. The results showed that wavelet frame based change detection method yielded better accuracy results compared to other change detection methods like PCA, Change Vector Analysis.

Do & Vetterli (2005) reported that contourlet transform gave an efficient directional multi resolution image representation. It represented the images having abundant directional selectivity.

Katsigiannis & Keramidas (2010) reported the texture representation scheme on thyroid ultrasound images to detect the hypoechoic and isoechoic thyroid nodules, which presented the highest malignancy risk. Texture representation scheme is an efficient method to detect malignancy with the maximum classification accuracy reached 95% for hypoechoic dataset, and 92% for isoechoic dataset. The results confirmed that contourlet based texture features could be successfully applied for the classification of different types of texture in ultrasound thyroid images.

Mahmoudi-Barmas & Kasaei (2008) proposed a novel method to extract salient edges from satellite images. For the image registration, various multi resolution transforms namely, wavelet, curvelet, complex wavelet and contourlet transform were used for the feature extraction. Higher performance in the extraction of efficient edges from satellite images was obtained in the contourlet transform.

Wang & Zhao (2010) discussed the contourlet transform and the support vector machine (SVM), which takes technological advantages of both SVM and the contourlet transform for feature extraction.

Femy & Victor (2014) reported the use of fundus database images to autodetect Glaucoma disease in the human eye which classified the input fundus images as normal or abnormal with very high accuracy. Discrete wavelet transform have less number of information and the features obtained are only in three directions (vertical, horizontal, diagonal). Contourlet transform yielded better resolution and more directions than discrete wavelet transform.

Li et al. (2013) proposed an unsupervised approach for change detection in multitemporal satellite images based on a novel detail-enhancing algorithm. The multi temporal source images were first used to generate the difference image, which were then decomposed into low-pass approximation and high-pass directional sub bands by the nonsubsampled contourlet transform. Experimental results demonstrated the superior performance of the proposed approach compared with several well-known change detection techniques.

Hamid Soltanian Zede et al. (2004) evaluated and compared the performance of four different texture feature extraction methods namely conventional shape quantifiers, co-occurence based method of Harlick, wavelet transform and multiwavelet transform for classification of mammogram images. Among this the multiwavelet based method outperformed the other three methods.

Ramakrishnan & Selven (2007) proposed an approach based on muliwavelets and singular value decomposition. The classifications were carried out using probabilistic neural network. Performance of this approach was compared to the wavelet domain. Multiwavelet based texture feature gave better results.

Kavitha Anandrao & Kale (2012) proposed GHM based texture features for IRIS recognition. The experimental results indicated that this type of features achieved higher recognition efficiency and stronger robustness.

Abdullah Al jumah et al. (2013) proposed a various non linear thresholding algorithms such as hard, soft, universal, modified universal were applied in different multiwavelets. The experimental results showed that CL multiwavelets in combination with modified universal thresholding gave better accuracy results.

Tarik Ismael et al. (2013) proposed stationary multiwavelet transform for face recognition. Stationary multiwavelet transform features increased the recognition rate compared to Histogram based method and principal component analysis.

An Zhiyong et al. (2014) proposed a new retrieval algorithm based on spatial texture using GHM based Multiwavelets. Multiwavelets could depict more information from the subbands. Experimental results showed that this method gave better performance than looseness texture algorithm.

### 1.2.5 Literature on Feature Reduction

The practical Pattern Recognition problem deals with a classification function obtained by an inductive learning algorithm that connects a given input pattern to one of the existing classes of the system. Each input pattern consists of features that can differentiate one class of pattern from the other in a precise and reliable way unlike the raw way of representation. But the inclusion of additional feature beyond a certain point leads to degradation but not to better performance. Additionally the selection of features to represent the patterns also influences several aspects of the problem such as accuracy, required learning time and necessary number of samples.

Cetin et al. (2004) reported that the level of contributions of multi-temporal and multi-sensor data together with their principal components for Maximum Likelihood and Artificial Neural Network classifiers.

Fauvel et al. (2006) reported that KPCA has a pre-processing step to extract relevant feature for classification and to prevent from the Hughes phenomenon.

Borges et al. (2007) reported that most commonly used feature selection and reduction algorithms like Jeffries-Matusita distance was used to determine the best subset of features and some spectral transformations such as Segmented Principal Component Analysis, Segmented Canonical Analysis,

Independent Component Analysis and Minimum Mean Squared Error were carried out to reduce the data dimensionality.

Sasikala et al. (2010) compared two linear dimension reduction methods namely Principal component analysis and linear discriminant analysis. The results showed that PCA based dimension reduction method recorded better performance with higher precision and recall values with lesser computational complexity than the LDA based method.

Koonsanit et al. (2012) reported that Principal Component Analysis (PCA) and Information gain methods were applied for hyper spectral images for band selection to reduce the spectral and spatial information without loss in any valuable details. A good result in terms of robust clustering was obtained when the tests were conducted from the small multi mission satellite images.

Sai et al. (2012*)* developed a spectrally segmented principal component analysis for accurately mapping the invasive plant species. Experimental results showed that the developed algorithm performs better than correlation based segmented transformation and conventional PCA.

### 1.2.6 Literature on Fuzzy Feature Classification

Sofyan (2005) reported fuzzy clustering method was implemented in statistical software package (XploRe), GIS (GRASS) and remote sensing (ERDAS) were used to classify and preset multi-spectral Land sat TM images. The investigations showed the superiority in the classification of underlying structures and patterns from the satellite images data unlike the conventional one.

Lizarazo & Barros (2011) proposed a Fuzzy approach for segmentation based classification. The results explained about the fuzzy image based region method that serves as a viable alternative to hard segmentation that performs well in differentiating the spectrally intermingled geographic objects.

Petcu et al. (2011) discussed about the efficiency of a parallelization strategy for the Fuzzy C-Means (FCM) algorithm in which for two FCM variants, the parallelization strategy has been extended by incorporating the spatial information.

Tsai et al. (2012) reported the suitability of bias-corrected fuzzy c-means algorithm with spatial information for image segmentation. The disadvantage of BCFCM is that it lacks enough robustness to noise and outliers for which few kernel versions of FCM with spatial constraints, such as KFCM_$S_1$, KFCM_$S_2$ and GKFCM.

Volpi et al. (2012) discussed the unsupervised kernel-based approach for change detection. Two different approaches based on different assumptions of the difference image were proposed. Among the two, the first one dealt with the difference image in the original space whereas the second one explained about the map that describes about the difference image directly in feature spaces. To standardize the parameters of the kernels, a new unsupervised cost function was used. The analysis of the two challenging change detection problems explains about the correctness, stability, and superiority of the proposed solution.

Zhiqiang Zhou & Jingjing Ma (2012) presented an unsupervised distribution-free change detection approach for synthetic aperture radar (SAR) images based on an image fusion strategy and a novel fuzzy clustering algorithm. A reformulated fuzzy local-information C-means clustering algorithm is proposed for classifying changed and unchanged regions in the fused difference image. The change detection results obtained by the improved fuzzy clustering algorithm exhibited lower error than its preexistences.

Soumi Ghosh & Sanjay Kumar Dubey (2013) analyzed the Fuzzy C-Means Clustering with K Means Clustering Algorithm. The experimental results showed that Fuzzy clustering gave better results compared to K-means clustering.

Somasundaram & Palaniswami (2015) reported the use of fuzzy c means algorithm for image segmentation in which spatial kernel Fuzzy C means algorithm was evaluated with various FCM algorithms. Kernel Fuzzy C means algorithm provided better efficiency and optimized results in image segmentation.

## 1.3 RESEARCH OBJECTIVES

The objective of this research is to investigate the most effective multi scale and multi directional transform based texture feature extraction techniques for improving the classification accuracy of satellite images. This goal is accomplished by studying the growth of Madurai Metropolitan Area, Tamilnadu using IRS LISS II, LISS III and LISS IV imagery.

The main objectives of the thesis are

- Design a texture based intelligent system using scalar wavelet and contourlet frame transform in satellite image classification

- Design a multiwavelet frame based feature extraction techniques to increase the classification accuracy compared to scalar wavelets
- Design a multiscale and multidirectional frame based features using multiwavelet and non subsampled contourlet frame to increase the classification accuracy of satellite images.

## 1.4 CONTRIBUTION OF THE THESIS

Investigation of the proposed land use/land cover using wavelet and contourlet frame based features for the segmentation of LISS II, LISS III, LISS IV Madurai imagery. The validity was tested using ground truth data and cluster validity measures. Investigation of the proposed multiwavelet frame based features and compared it with scalar wavelets for land use /land cover mapping.

Investigation of the proposed combination of multiwavelet and contourlet frame based features (MCT) for land use/land cover mapping.

## 1.5 THESIS ORGANIZATION

The organization of the thesis as follows

Chapter 1 of the thesis provides an introduction to remote sensing, stages of remote sensing, optical remote sensing, applications and challenges of remote sensing, importance of land use /land cover mapping, list of Indian remote sensing satellites and cites the different works which have been carried out in the area, objectives and contribution of the thesis.

Chapter 2 provides the details about study area and the data used in this work. It also represents the different methods used in this research wavelet frame transform, contourlet frame transform, multiwavelet frame transform, principal component analysis and Guassian kernel fuzzy clustering algorithm (GKFCM).

Chapter 3 presents the accuracy assessment using ground truth data and cluster validity measures.

Chapter 4 presents the performance of different contourlet and scalar wavelet frame based feature extraction techniques for the classification of satellite images.

Chapter 5 discusses the performance analysis of scalar wavelet and multiwavelet frame based features for classification of satellite images.

Chapter 6 details the combination of multiwavelet and contourlet frame based features for improving classification accuracy of satellite images

Chapter 7 discusses the performance of the proposed methods in Chapter IV, Chapter V & Chapter VI

Chapter 8 gives the conclusion with a summary of the outcomes of the research work and future research issues that arose from the investigations carried out are discussed.

# CHAPTER 2

# STUDY AREA, TOOLS AND TECHNIQUES USED

This chapter provides the information about study area Madurai city with their metrological attributes and land cover details. The different tools and techniques used for processing the satellite images were presented in the remaining chapters. The remaining chapter details about image geo referencing, wavelet transform and its types, steps to perform the contourlet transform, analysis of multi wavelet transform, feature reduction using Principal Component Analysis (PCA), feature mapping using different kernel functions and feature classification using fuzzy c means algorithm.

## 2.1 STUDY AREA

The selected area of this research is the Madurai District, located in Tamilnadu state of India shown in Figure 2.1. It is the second largest population in 32 districts of the state of Tamilnadu. Madurai city serves as a district head quarters. It is a historical city and referred as the gateway of south Tamilnadu and it is considered as the capital of southern districts. It is one of the mini metros in India.

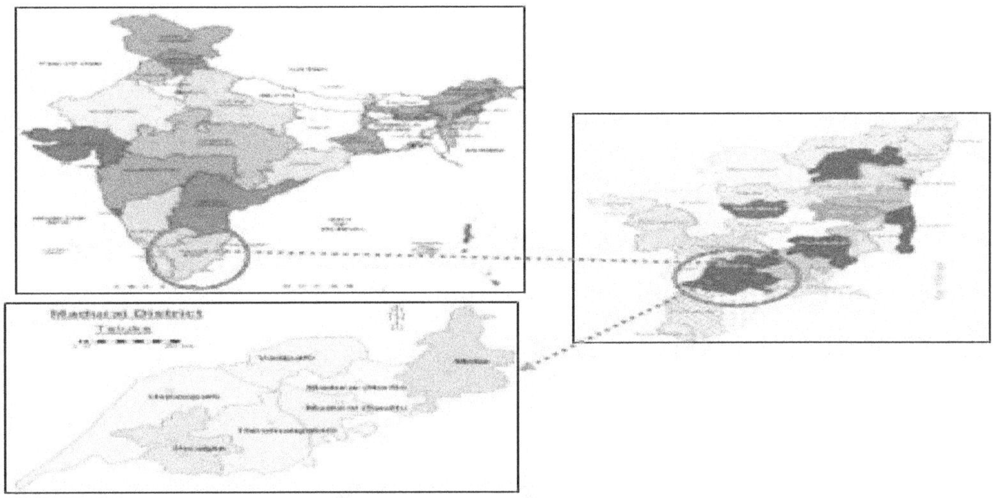

(Source - http://www.madurai.tn.nic.in/mdu_tlks.gif)

**Figure 2.1 Madurai district map**

The city is known as the Athens of the east. The geographical location of Madurai district North latitude between 9°30.00 and 10°30.00 and East latitude between 77°00.00 and 78°30.00 . The district is located 489 Km north towards state capital Chennai. The district shares its border with Dindigul district to North, Sivagangai district to East, Virudhunagar district to South. The present area of the district is 3741.73 square kilometres. As per the population census of India, Madurai district had a population of about 30, 38, 252. The urbanization percentage in Madurai district is about 65%.

### 2.1.1 Metrological Attributes of Madurai

Madurai district comprises of 13 taluks namely Thiruparankundram, T.Kallupatti, Tirumangalam, Kalligudi, Sedapatti, Usilampatti, Vadipatti, Melur, Madurai West, Madurai East, Kottampatti, Alanganallur and sellampatti. According to these taluks Madurai East, Madurai West, Thirumangalam, Thiruparankundram taluk having more urbanization. Vadipatti, Usilampatti, Alanganallur, Kottampatti taluk having more hilly and vegetation areas. Water bodies like Vaigai River, Madukulam pond, Nilayur pond are situated in Madurai East and Thiruparankundram taluks. The larger towns from the Madurai district are Melur, Avaniapuram, Thirumangalam, and Usilampatti. The climate is moderate with no extremes. The Madurai city covers 51.9 square kilometres in Madurai district. The land cover features of this study area include bare land, urban, vegetation, water body and Hilly area.

### 2.1.2 Land Cover details

#### 2.1.2.1 Urban

In Madurai district Thiruparankundram, Madurai East, Madurai West, Thirumangalam are the four taluks in Madurai district having more urbanization, The urban area consists of areas like buildings, cities, towns, villages, transportation, shopping centers, industrial, highways and commercial complexes, residential areas, concrete occurring in and around and roads.

#### 2.1.2.2 Vegetation

The vegetation class includes cropland, pastures, orchards, groves, vineyards, nurseries, grasses, grass like plants, forbs the heavy and sparse vegetation areas in the image. Major crops in Madurai district are Paddy (Dhan), Maize (Makka), Pearl Millet, Black Gram, Cowpea, Green Gram, Pigeon pea, Castor, Groundnut and Cotton.

#### 2.1.2.3 Water Bodies

Water category consists of streams, canals, lakes, reservoirs, bays and estuaries. Vaigai River is the main river that feeds in to the Madurai city. Periyar dam and vaigai dam reservoir irrigates most of the cultivable lands in the city. Major Ponds like Avaniapuram, Thiruparankundram, and Madakulam supports the water supply in Madurai city. Water area reflected by the earth having the very low electromagnetic radiation.

#### 2.1.2.4 Waste Lands

Boulders, rocky outcrop, relief, stone quarry, uncultivable wastelands are categorized into wastelands. A significant portion (34.6%) of the land falls under the category of non available for cultivation and fallow lands. The city has waste lands in the North West, South West and South East part of the city.

#### 2.1.2.5 Hilly

Hilly areas consist of bare exposed rocks with high grass, stripe mines, quarries and gravel pits. Madurai district consists of hilly areas like Alagar kovil, Thiruparankundram, Pasumalai etc

## 2.2 TOOLS USED

System Information:

- System: Lenovo
- RAM: 4 GB RAM
- Hard disk: 500 GB
- Processor: i3 processor
- Processor Speed: 3.0 GHZ
- Monitor: Liquid crystal display 18.5 inch

Softwares used:

MATLAB

The name MATLAB stands for Matrix Laboratory. MATLAB has evolved over a period of years with getting the input from many users .MATLAB is a high-performance tool for technical computing. It integrates computation, visualization and programming in an user friendly environment where problems and solutions were expressed in familiar mathematical notation. Typical uses include mathematical computation, developing algorithms, data acquisition, prototyping, data analysis, data exploration and visualization, scientific analysis and engineering applications.

MATLAB 12b

MATLAB 12b (version 8.0) has wide range of applications, including image and signal processing, communications, control design, test and measurement, financial modeling applications and analysis of computational information. Add-on toolboxes (collections of special-purpose MATLAB functions, available separately) extends the MATLAB environment to solve particular classes of problems in these application areas. MATLAB 12b provides a number of features for documenting and sharing user work. MATLAB is a high-level programming language tool that enables scientists and engineers to move quickly from idea to implementation and can be easily integrated with other languages and applications.

MATLAB is an interactive system in which basic data element is an array that does not require dimensioning.The software package has been commercially available and considered as a standard tool at most university and industries worldwide. This allows us to solve many technical computing problems, especially those with matrix and vector formulations.

ENVI

ENVI (an acronym for "Environment for Visualizing Images") is a software application used to process and analyze geospatial imagery. It is commonly used by remote sensing professionals and image analysts.

ENVI combines advanced image processing and proven geospatial technology to help us to extract meaningful information from all kinds of data and to make better decisions.

## 2.3 DATA USED

Four satellite images taken by Indian remote sensing satellites are taken for analysis. The input Madurai district images are shown in Figure 2.2.The details of the Madurai image is shown in Table 2.1.

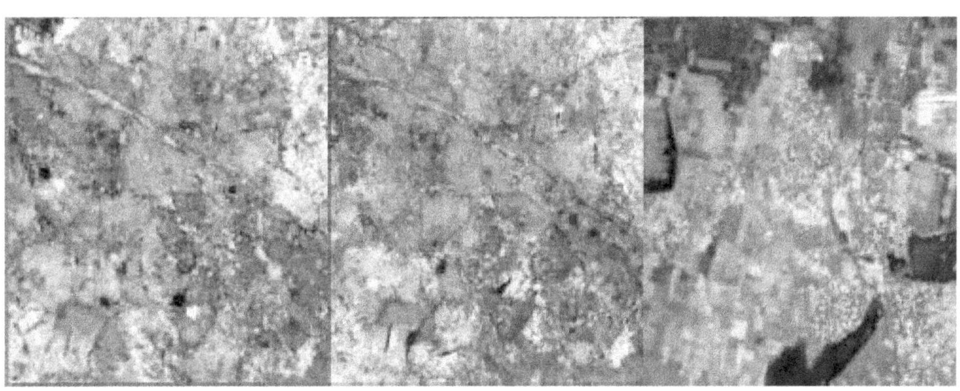

(a) (b) (c)

(d)

(Source - National Remote Sensing Agency, Hyderabad)

**Figure 2.2 Madurai (a) LISS II (b) LISS III (c) LISS IV(i) (d) LISS IV(ii) Images**

**Table 2.1 Details of the Madurai image**

| | **Image 1-LISS II** | **Image 2-LISS III** | **Image 3-LISS IV** |
|---|---|---|---|
| Date of acquisition | 4thMarch, 1996 | 19thMarch, 2004 | 25thApril, 2009 |

The satellite data of the Madurai city used here is captured by means of LISS II, LISS III, and LISS IV sensor .The sensor details are given below

The scene details of the area are,

LISS II:

- Satellite/Sensor : IRS 1A/1B
- Resolution : 36 m
- Swath Width :74 km

Spectral Characteristics of LISS II are,

- Band 1(Blue) :0.45-.052μm
- Band 2(Green) :0.52-0.59μm
- Band 3(Red) :0.62-0.68μm
- Band 4(Near IR) :0.77-0.86μm

The scene details of LISS III are

- Satellite/Sensor : IRS 1C/1D
- Resolution : 23.5 m
- Swath Width :142 km

Spectral Characteristics of LISS III are,

- Band 2(Green) :0.52-0.59μm
- Band 3(Red) :0.2-0.68μm
- Band 3(Near IR) :0.77-0.86μm
- Band 5(Mid IR) :1.55-1.70μm

The scene details of the LISS IV are,

- Satellite/Sensor : IRS P6/LISS IV
- Resolution : 5.8 m
- Swath Width :24-70 km

Spectral Characteristics of LISS IV are,

- Band 2 (green) : 0.52~0.59 μm
- Band 3 (red) : 0.62~0.68 μm
- Band 4 (near-Infrared) : 0.77~0.86 μm

## 2.4 IMAGE GEO-REFERENCING

Geo-referencing is a process of associating the satellite images with spatial locations. It is most commonly used to describe the process of associating a physical map with spatial locations. It is commonly represented using a coordinate reference system related to a geodetic reference system such as WGS 84. For geo referencing, an image is first used to establish ground control points. Then, the known geographic coordinates were used as input to these ground control points. The other coordinate system was then chosen and the different projection parameters were selected to minimize the residuals. Residuals are the difference between the actual coordinate system and ground control points. Various GIS tools like ARCGIS, ERDAS, ENVI Geomatica and Arcmap were used for geo referencing.

The Madurai district images were geo-referenced using Survey of India topographic sheets 58 K/l, 1:50,000 and four 58 K/l SW, SE, NW, NE 1:25,000 scale were used as reference data ground control points (GCPs) collection and validation. The standard errors were below 0.5 pixels along the X and Y directions.

## 2.5 NEED FOR TEXTURE ANALYSIS

Texture describes the surface and structural properties of an image. Texture can be of smooth, coarse, grainy, stippled, fine and lumped. It is generally used to classify the remote sensing imagery with diverse landscapes and that have high spectral heterogeneity. It can be seen in all multispectral scanner images which are obtained from aircraft or satellite platforms. Texture is an important information in remote sensing and significant base of interpretation by manual work and computer. One immediate application of image texture is the recognition of image regions using texture properties.

Remote sensing data shows different textures for different regions. For example, forest area shows different texture from urban area. So, textures can be used for remotely sensed data classification.

Texture analysis refers to acquire the texture character through some image processing technology, which then obtains quantitative or qualitative description of texture. Texture can be thought as a structure consisting of a large number of more or less ordered similar elements or patterns. In the field of image processing, texture is seen as a rich source of information about the nature of physical surfaces and the analysis of texture falls, broadly into three areas:

1. Segmentation: The portioning of image into regions consisting of single texture.
2. Classification: Labelling a region with a single texture
3. Shape: Using textural information to derive three dimensional surface geometry from a two dimensional scene.

The work undertaken in this research falls largely into the area of texture classification. Texture analysis is considered to be a difficult image processing task for a number of reasons, including:

1. The boundary between texture regions is marked by a change in the distribution of image intensities rather than a simple change in the mean intensity.
2. Although textures can often be seen to have a particular orientation it is not always desirable that this should affect the classification of the texture. In some applications a change in texture orientation is interpreted as the start of a new region

(for instance to identify three dimensional surfaces within an image). Within the framework of this project, however, a non-directional texture measure is desirable.

3. Texture classification should be independent of the image intensity. For example, regions of pure black and pure white have the same texture but at a different intensity.

The major applications of texture analysis include:

- Classification of remote sensing imagery
- Analysis of satellite or aerial imagery
- Content-based retrieval from image databases
- Document analysis
- Biometric person authentication
- Scene analysis for robot navigation
- Texture synthesis for computer graphics and animation

Texture Features are generally a piece of information. Texture feature extraction is the process of extracting the feature set that is useful for solving computational task for specific applications. The texture can be described by parameters usually denoted as features. The basic assumption for most filtering approaches is that the energy distribution in the frequency domain identifies a texture. Hence, if the frequency spectrum of the textured image is decomposed into a sufficient number of subbands, the spectral energy signatures of different textures are different. Texture Feature extraction is the process of generating textures to be used in the selection and classification tasks.

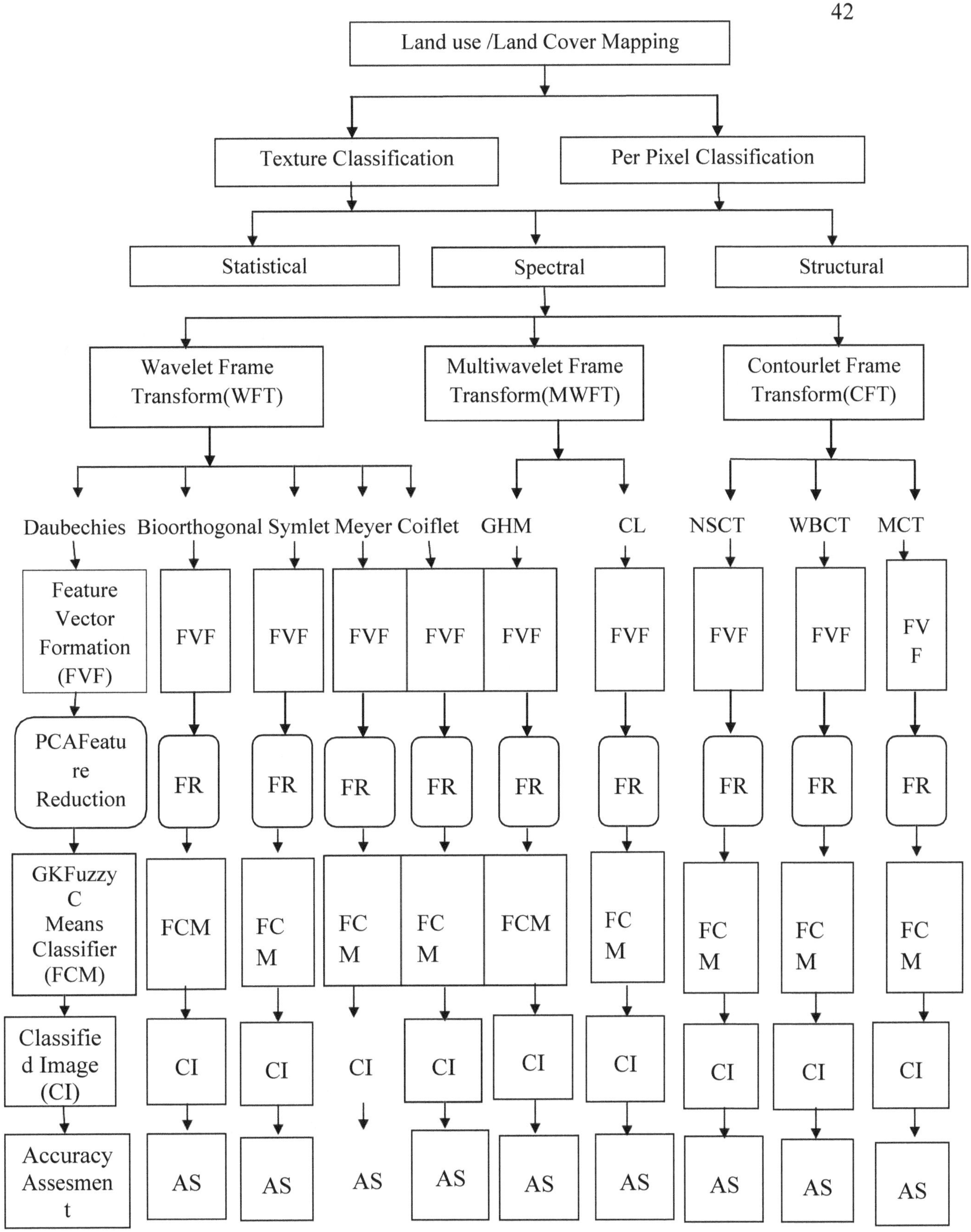


**Figure 2.3 Work flow**

Statistical, structural and spectral based texture feature extraction techniques were widely followed. Statistical approaches yield characterizations of as smooth, coarse and grainy. Structural techniques discuss with the arrangement of the different image primitives such as the description of features based on regularly spaced parallel lines. Spectral techniques were based on properties of the Fourier spectrum primarily to detect global periodicity in an image by identifying high-energy, narrow peaks in the spectrum. Wavelet transform is one of the spectral based feature extraction technique and multi-resolution analytical tool for spatial frequency feature extraction. The workflow of the research is shown in Figure 2.3.

## 2.6 WAVELET TRANSFORM

Wavelet transform is a multiresolution analytical tool for texture classification which is also capable of compressing and denoising an image without substantial degradation of the original image. Wavelet packet and Wavelet frame transforms were the advanced methods used for texture feature extraction. But compared to wavelet packet transform, down sampling operation is not performed in wavelet frame transform which is also called as Stationary Wavelet Transform.

### 2.6.1 Stationary Wavelet Transform

The stationary wavelet transform is otherwise referred to as undecimated wavelet transform. This wavelet transform was used to avoid the lack of translation invariance in the discrete wavelet transform which is accomplished by removing the downsamplers and upsamplers in the discrete wavelet transform and then upsampling the filter coefficients by a factor of $2^{(j-1)}$ in the $j^{th}$ level of the discrete wavelet transform algorithm.

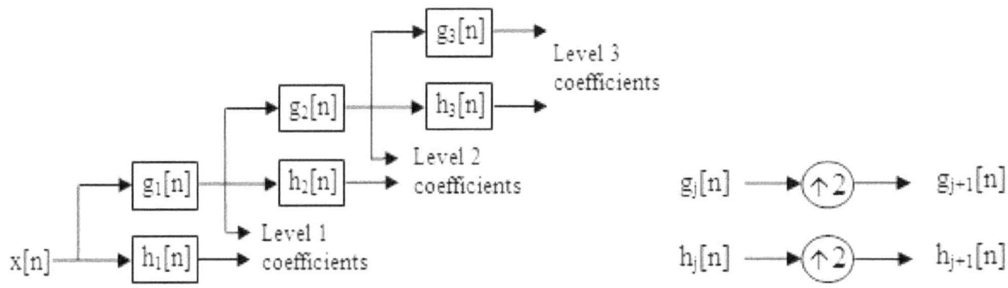


a) b)

**Figure 2.4 Filter-bank structure of 1D- SWT a) 3 level SWT filter bank b) SWT filters**

The approximation and detail co-efficient at each level of matrix size is same as that of original with maximum number of co-efficient in the stationary wavelet transform. The translation invariance property is a vital component of feature-extraction applications.

Figure 2.4 a & b shows the filter-bank structure for the 3 level SWT, where h and g represent the low-pass and high-pass filter respectively. An image x(n) was decomposed into four sub band images after going through one stage of decomposition process. The four sub band images consist of one average information image and three detail information. The approximation image is actually the low-frequency detail image contains the information of specific scale and orientation. The detail images were used to derive more number of texture features in the input images whereas the approximation image was used for higher level of decomposition in the input image.

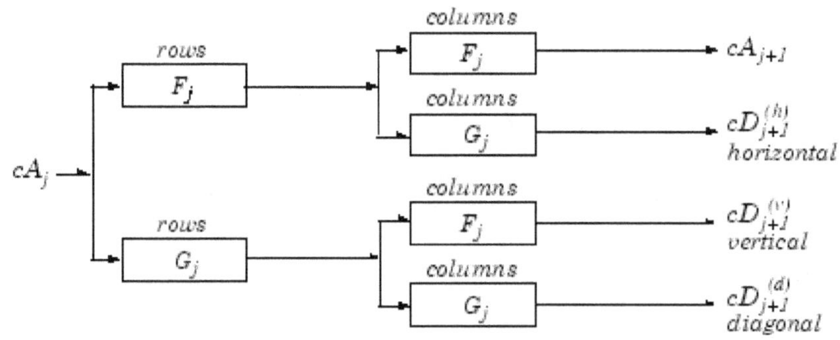


**Figure 2.5 Decomposition process of 2D-SWT**

The simplest way of generating the two dimensional wavelet transform is to apply two 1D transforms separately. This transform is called dyadic wavelet transform. To compute dyadic wavelet transform of an image, we should apply one dimensional wavelet transform to both dimensions of an image separately. The decomposition of approximation co-efficients at level j with four components is the result of two-dimensional stationary wavelet transform, the approximation component at level j+1, and the detail component in three orientations (horizontal, vertical, and diagonal). The following Figure 2.5 describes the basic 2D-SWT decomposition steps for images where F and G are the low pass and high pass filters.

### 2.6.2 Wavelet Families

Wavelet families vary in terms of several important properties. Examples include:

- Support of the wavelet in time and frequency and rate of decay.
- Symmetry or asymmetry of the wavelet. The accompanying perfect reconstruction filters have linear phase.

- Number of vanishing moments. Wavelets with increasing numbers of vanishing moments result in sparse representations for a large class of signals and images.
- Regularity of the wavelet. Smoother wavelets provide sharper frequency resolution. Additionally, iterative algorithms for wavelet construction converge faster.
- Existence of a scaling function, φ.

The popular wavelet families used for remote sensing applications is described below

Daubechies wavelet

The Daubechies wavelets, based on the work of Ingrid Daubechies, a family of orthogonal wavelets defining a discrete wavelet transform and characterized by a maximal number of vanishing moments for some given support. With each wavelet type of this class, there is a scaling function which generates an orthogonal multiresolution analysis. The scaling and wavelet coefficients of the Daubechies wavelet is shown in Figure 2.6 a & b.

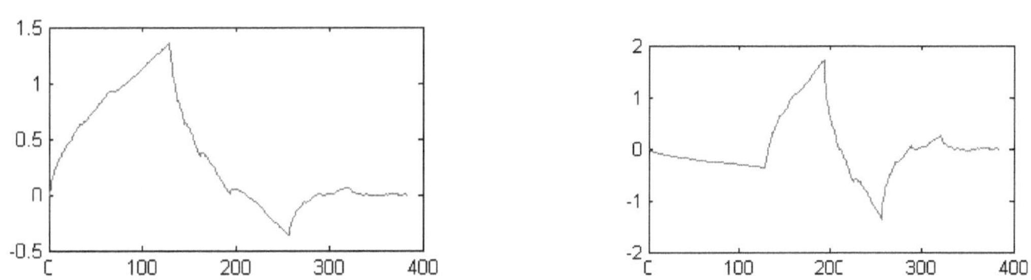


**Figure 2.6 a) Scaling function b) Wavelet function**

Coiflet Wavelet

Coiflets are discrete wavelets designed by Ingrid Daubechies, at the request of Ronald Coifman, to have scaling functions with vanishing moments. The wavelet is near symmetric; their wavelet functions have N/3 vanishing moments and scaling functions (N/3) -1, and have been used in many applications using Calderón-Zygmund Operators. The Scaling and wavelet functions of the coiflet wavelet is shown in Figure 2.7 a & b.

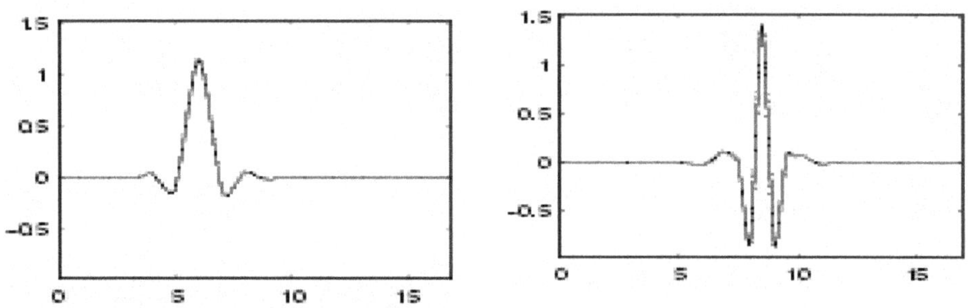


**Figure 2.7 a) Scaling function b) Wavelet function**

Symlet Wavelet

In applied mathematics, symlet wavelets are a family of wavelets. They are a modified version of Daubechies wavelets with increased symmetry. The scaling and wavelet functions of the symlet wavelet is shown in Figure 2.8 a & b.

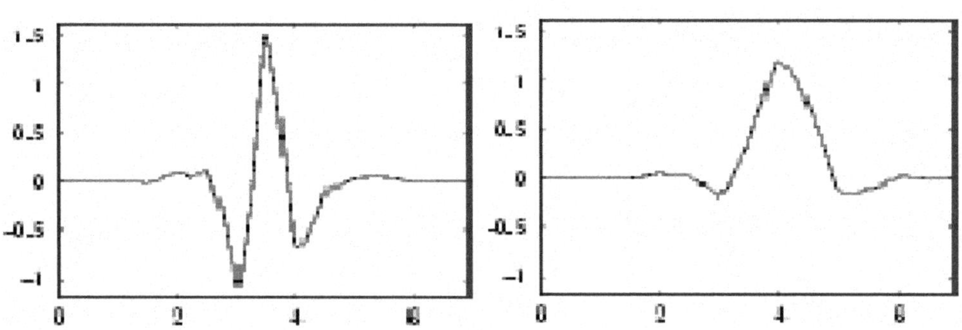


**Figure 2.8 a) Scaling function b) Wavelet function**

Biorthogonal Wavelet

A biorthogonal wavelet is a wavelet where the associated wavelet transform is invertible but not necessarily orthogonal. Designing biorthogonal wavelets allows more degrees of freedom than orthogonal wavelets. One additional degree of freedom is the possibility to construct symmetric wavelet functions. The scaling and wavelet coefficients of the bio orthogonal wavelet is shown in Figure 2.9 a & b.

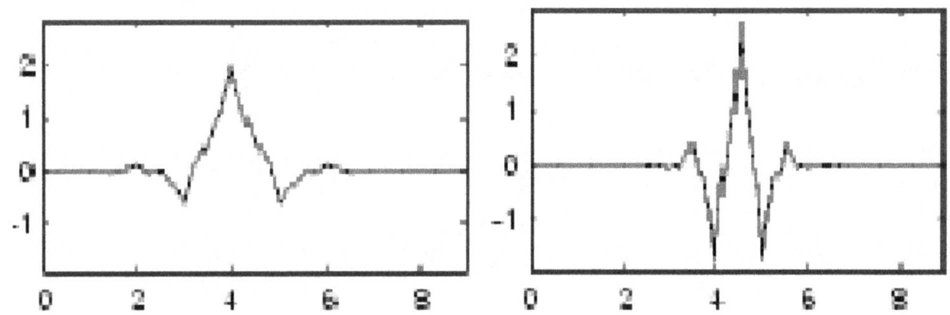


**Figure 2.9 a) Scaling function b) Wavelet function**

Meyer Wavelet

Proposed by Yves Meyer is an orthogonal wavelet, Meyer wavelet is defined in frequency domain in terms of function $\nu$.It is infinitely differentiable with infinite support. The Scaling and wavelet functions of the Meyer wavelet is shown in Figure 2.10 a & b.

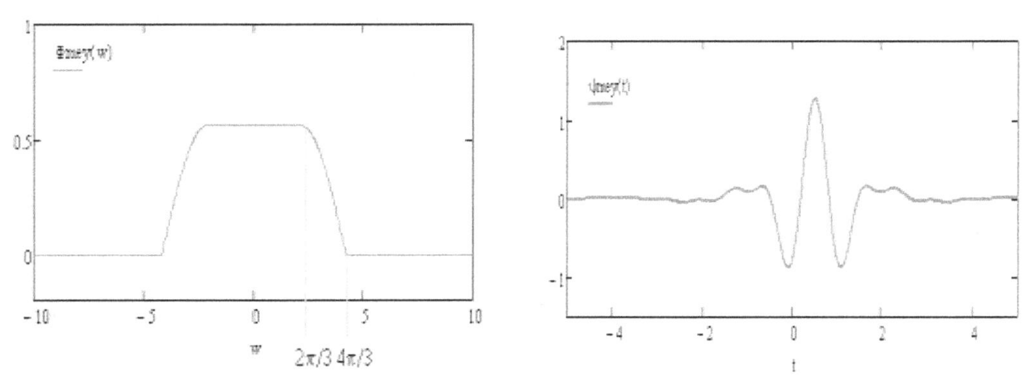


**Figure 2.10 a) Scaling function b) Wavelet function**

## 2.7 CONTOURLET TRANSFORM

Contourlets provides a sparse expansion of images having smooth contours. The contourlet transform has a fast implementation based on a Laplacian Pyramid decomposition followed by directional filter banks applied on each band pass sub band as shown in Figure 2.11.

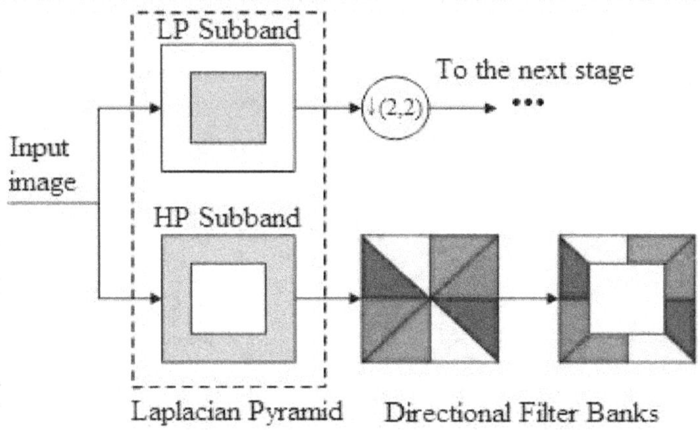


**Figure 2.11 Contourlet based image decomposition**

The directional filter banks can be efficiently implemented using l level binary tree decomposition and it leads to $2^l$ sub bands with wedge shaped frequency, where l is the directional sub bands. A directional filter bank was applied on the input images and the resulting image is a multidirectional tight frame composed of different contour segments. This overcomed the challenges of wavelet transform. Compared to the wavelet transform, Contourlet offers a richer set of directions and shapes and thus they are effective in capturing smooth contours and edges at any orientation.

### 2.7.1 Laplacian Pyramid

In the first stage of Contourlet, the Laplacian pyramid was used to achieve the multiscale decomposition. The Laplacian pyramid at each level generates a downsampled lowpass version of the source image and the difference between the source image and the downsample lowpass image, resulting in a highpass image. The structure of the Laplacian pyramid is shown in Figure 2.12, where H and G are the analysis and synthesis filters, respectively, and M is the sampling matrix. It should be noted that in multidimensional filter banks, the sampling operation was represented by the sampling matrices. That is, the source signal x[n] downsampled by M will become

$$x_d[n] = x_d[Mn]$$

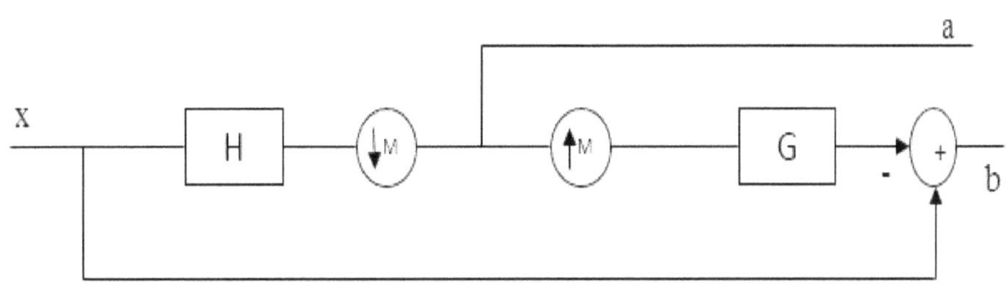


**Figure 2.12 Laplacian Pyramid filter structure**

The downsampled lowpass version of the source signal a can be tied to the next level Laplacian pyramid, which will forms an iterated structure.

### 2.7.2 Directional Filter Banks

The directional filter banks (DFB) were used to derive the high frequency subbands with diverse directionality. The DFB can be efficiently implemented via l-level binary tree decomposition that leads to $2^l$ subbands with wedge-shaped frequency supports as shown in Figure 2.13 a. The directionality of the frequency supports can be controlled by the tree-structure directional filter banks, which is shown in Figure 2.13 b. Since the Laplacian pyramid and the directional filter banks are obtained, we can combine them to accomplish the contourlet transform. This is a multiscale and directional decomposition using a combination of a Laplacian pyramid and directional filter banks. The highpass images are from the Laplacian pyramid and fed into the directional filter banks so the high frequency directional information can be captured.

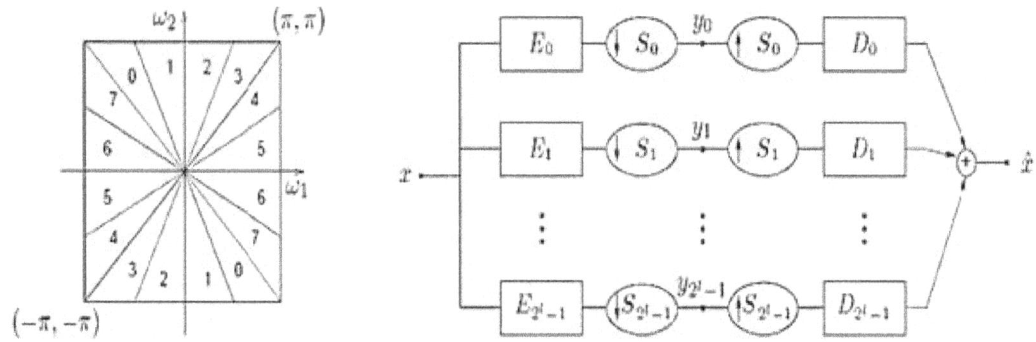


a) b)

**Figure 2.13 Directional Filter Bank a) Subbands with wedge shaped b) Tree structure directional filter banks**

The coarse image from the Laplacian pyramid is downsampled and fed into another stage of the contourlet filter banks.

## 2.8 MULTIWAVELET TRANSFORM

Multiwavelet outperforms the scalar wavelets by satisfying several mathematical properties simultaneously. Four properties are desirable for the transform bases in image processing using transform techniques. They are

- Finite Impulse Response
- Symmetry for linear phase
- Orthogonality for perfect reconstruction and
- Compact support.

Scalar wavelet transform fails to possess all these properties simultaneously. Properties like orthogonality and compact support is to provide perfect reconstruction while preserving the length, linear phase symmetry ensure good performance at the boundaries and vanishing moments provides higher order approximation. Multiwavelets also offer better energy compaction. When a Multiresolution analysis is generated using multiple scaling function and multiple wavelet function it gives rise to notion of multiwavelets.

Multiwavelet system possess one or more scaling and wavelet function. A multiwavelet system with r scaling and r wavelet functions is said to have multiplicity r. When r = 1, i.e., one scaling function and one wavelet function, then the multiwavelet system reduces to the scalar wavelets here we consider r = 2. The 2x2 matrix filters in multiwavelet filter bank requires vector inputs. The 2- dimensional wavelet transform has been implemented as two separable 1- dimensional transforms. This transformation is called pre-processing. Pre-processing process must be accompanied by an appropriate prefiltering operation that depends on the spectral characteristics of the multiwavelet filters. However, some multiwavelets obviate the pre-filtering operation due to certain desirable properties of their basis functions those multiwavelets are called balanced multiwavelets.

### 2.8.1 Multiresolution Analysis

A multi resolution analysis of $L^2(R)$ space generated using multiple scaling functions and wavelet functions gives rise to the notion of multiwavelets. The multiscaling function is given by the vector $\Phi(t) = [\Phi_1(t), \Phi_2(t),. \Phi_r(t)]^T$ and it satisfies two scale equation

$$\phi(t) = \sqrt{2} \sum_{k=-\infty}^{\infty} H_k \phi(2t - k) \tag{2.1}$$

where H[*k*] is a sequence of r x r matrices of real coefficients.

where the matrix filter H[k] has l 2×2 matrix coefficients; the kth matrix coefficient is given by

$$H[k] = \begin{bmatrix} h0(2k) & h0(2k+1) \\ h1(2k) & h1(2k+1) \end{bmatrix} \tag{2.2}$$

such that $\sum_k h0(k)^2 = 1$ and $\sum_k h1(k)^2 = 1$. The wavelet equation also holds the same except that the wavelet function is a multiwavelet function generated by r wavelet functions. The multiwavelet function is given by the vector $\Psi(t) = [\Psi_1(t), \Psi_2(t), \ldots. \Psi_r(t)]^T$. Wavelet equation is given by equation where G[*k*] is of same dimension as H[*k*]

$$\varphi(t) = \sqrt{2} \sum_{k=-\infty}^{\infty} G_k \phi(2t - k) \tag{2.3}$$

where the matrix filter G[k] has l 2×2 matrix coefficients; the kth matrix coefficient is given by

$$G[k] = \begin{bmatrix} g0(2k) & g0(2k+1) \\ g1(2k) & g1(2k+1) \end{bmatrix} \tag{2.4}$$

such that $\sum_k g0(k)^2 = 1$ and $\sum_k g1(k)^2 = 1$. Where $\{H_k\}$ and $\{G_k\}$ are the low pass and high pass matrix filters i.e., $\{H_k\}$ and $\{G_k\}$ are 2x2 matrices, thus for convolution they need to be convolved with two rows of data. The pre-processing should not destroy orthogonality and symmetry of the bases. To provide a solution to this problem is simply to repeat the input which is equivalent to oversampling. Another solution is to perform critical sampling by splitting the input into two polyphase components. The repeated row processing can generate more information than the critical sampling. By oversampling method we add redundancy to the output which is desirable for feature extraction techniques.

Similar to a scalar filter bank, the low pass branches in a multiwavelets should preserve some polynomial inputs while the highpass branches should completely annihilate them. The annihilation property of the high pass branches in multiwavelet filter bank depends on its approximation order. In order to hold the preservation property, the polynomial inputs should be given signals of the lowpass branch.

## 2.9 FEATURE REDUCTION

The features that do not contribute to the discrimination of classes by assessing some criteria in feature reduction. Feature reduction should be done based on methods devised to allow the relative worth of features to be assessed in a quantitative and rigorous way and cannot be performed indiscriminately. It aims to improve the classification performance to remove the redundant information substantially without sacrificing significant information. This redundancy of the information was removed by applying algorithm-Principal component analysis (PCA).

The entire principal components transformation can be divided into three steps.

- Derivation of covariance matrix
- Computation of eigen vectors and
- Linear transformation of the data set

PCA has been applied to image data sets comprising bands from two or more dates. Let there are *n* number of features for an image of size MxN. So the feature vector x of the image is of dimension MN x n where the each column represents the features of the respective pixel in the image.

The mean vector of the population is defined as

$$m_x = \frac{1}{M}\sum_{k=1}^{M} x_k \tag{2.5}$$

The covariance matrix of the population is defined as

$$C_k = \sum_{k=1}^{M} x_k x_k^T - m_x m_x^T \tag{2.6}$$

For the covariance matrix $C_x$ which is real and symmetric, we find a set of n orthonormal Eigen vectors. Let $e_i$ and i=1,2……….,n, be the eigen vectors and corresponding eigen values of $C_x$,arranged in descending order so that for j=1,2…..,n-1. Let A be a matrix whose rows are formed from the eigen vectors of $C_x$, ordered so that the First row of A represents the largest eigen value of eigen vector whereas the last row represents the lowest eigen value of the eigen vector.The output eigen channels produced by the principal component transformation have a large dynamic range, especially the first few layers which pack most of the information.

## 2.10 FEATURE CLASSIFICATION

Texture classification is a basic task in the process of satellite image analysis which involves a method of identification of the different texture regions based on the corresponding features. This method can be clustering or classification of remote sensing image to a land cover class. The overall objective of image classification procedures is to automatically categorize all pixels in an image into land cover classes or themes. It is nothing but assigning the decision making process to the computer with or without the help of a prior information.

### 2.10.1 Types of Classification

Image Classification is the process of grouping similar pixels and forming a class. This method can be a clustering or a classification approach. There are different types of classification. They are as follows.

1. Supervised Classification
2. Unsupervised Classification

The supervised classification combines all pixels in an image into different classes. This combination requires an analysis of the spectral properties of surface features present in the input image based on mathematical decision rule. The main aim of supervised classification is

- The identity and location of some of the land cover types are known a priori through a combination of fieldwork, air photo interpretation and personal experience.
- The image analyst "supervises" the pixel categorization process by specifying for a computer algorithm, numerical descriptors of various land cover types in a scene.
- The image analyst guides the classification by identifying areas on an image that are known to belong to given categories (calibration of decision rules).

The steps involved in supervised classification are,

- Explaining the information classes
- Training, calibration and site selection that involves locating the areas of similar identity in the digital image
- Deriving the statistical procedure to be followed ie. To define the novel spectral characteristics.
- Stage of classification in which unknown pixels will be allotted with patriculat information classes
- Validation and assessment of accuracy
- Final stage of output.

The main aim of the unsupervised classification (UC) is

It is the identification of natural groups, or structures within multispectral data. It does not use training data for individual information classes as the basis for classification;

- image pixels were examined and aggregated into a number of spectral classes based on natural clustering in multi-dimensional space;
- UC is the definition, identification, labeling and mapping of natural spectral classes.

The steps involved in Unsupervised Classification are

- Definition of minimum and maximum number of categories to be generated by the particular classification algorithm (based on an analyst"s knowledge or user requirements).

- Random selection of pixels to form cluster centers.
- Algorithm then finds distances between pixels and forms initial estimates of cluster centers as permitted by user defined criteria.
- As pixels are added to the initial estimates, new class means are calculated. This is an iterative process until the mean does not change significantly from one iteration to the next.

The advantages of unsupervised classification is

- No extensive/detailed a priori knowledge of the region is required (nature of the knowledge required for UC differs from that required for supervised classification)
- Minimize human errors/biases (fewer decisions by analyst)
- Produces more uniform classes
- Spectrally distinct classes present in the data may not have initially been apparent to the analyst.

The supervised classification highly depends on the training data. The user should be an expert and require some prior knowledge for the selection of good training data. This is not possible in all situations. So, Unsupervised classification is becoming increasingly popular in many areas that requires classification.

### 2.10.2 Need for Fuzzy Classification

The problem is the impreciseness in the boundaries between geographical entities, and/or heterogeneity within a texture in one class that causes spectral overlap with texture in other classes. Classical set theory / hard classification decision rule belongs to one class only. Fuzzy set theory / membership function (a pixel may have partial membership in several classes) able to obtain information on the various constituent classes within a “mixed” pixel accounts for uncertainty in class assignment. K-means clustering is belongs to hard classification technique, so it cannot handle data points that are close to more than one cluster. Using fuzzy logic the above problem can be overcomed. One possible fuzzy clustering is the use of fuzzy C-means clustering.

### 2.10.3 Feature Mapping

Kernel functions were used to provide a simple bridge from linearity to non-linearity for algorithms. The higher dimensional feature space was generated by applying kernel on the reduced feature set.

Different kernel functions such as linear kernel, polynomial kernel, logarithmic kernel and Gaussian RBF kernel can be used to generate the higher dimensional feature space. The cost functions used to construct the kernel functions are given below.

Linear kernel

The Linear kernel is the simplest kernel function. It is given by the inner product <x,y> plus an optional constant **c**. Kernel algorithms using a linear kernel are often equivalent to their non-kernel counterparts.

$$k(x) = x_1^T x_2 + c \tag{2.7}$$

Polynomial kernel

The polynomial kernel otherwise referred as non-stationary kernel is widely used for the problems related to the normalized training data.

$$k(x) = (\alpha x_1^T x_2 + c)^d \tag{2.8}$$

Where, the slope alpha, the constant term c and the polynomial degree d are adjustable parameters.

Log kernel

The Log kernel seems to be particularly interesting for images, but is only conditionally positive definite.

$$k(x) = -\log \left\| x_2 - x_1 \right\|^d + 1 \tag{2.9}$$

Gaussian kernel

The Gaussian kernel is an example of radial basis function kernel. A higher dimensional feature space is generated by applying Gaussian kernel to the input data samples.

$$k(x) = \exp(-\| x_2 - x_1 \|^2 (2\sigma 2))a \tag{2.10}$$

Where, σ is the adjustable parameter.

The RBF kernel helps us to pick hyper spheres whereas linear kernels pick hyper planes only. For mappings, each kernel are not unique.

The Guassian Kernel Fuzzy classification algorithm is defined as given a dataset, X= {$x_1, \ldots, x_n$} ⊂ $R^P$, the original FCM algorithm partitions the dataset X into c fuzzy subsets by minimizing the following objective function

$$J_m(U,V) = \sum_{i=1}^{c}\sum_{k=1}^{n} u_{ik}^m \left\| x_k - v_i \right\|^2 \qquad (2.11)$$

where c defines the number of clusters, n is the number of data points, $u_{ik}$ represents the membership function of $x_k$ in class i, satisfying $\sum_{i=1}^{c} u_{ik} = 1$, m the quantity that controls the cluster fuzziness and v is the set of the cluster centers ($v_i \in R^p$). The function $J_m$ is minimized by an iterative algorithm.

Kernel fuzzy c-means (KFCM) algorithm define a nonlinear map as Φ: x → Φ(x) ∈*F*, where x ∈ X. X denotes the data space, and F the transformed feature space with higher even infinite dimension. KFCM minimizes the following objective function

$$J_m = 2\sum_{i=1}^{c}\sum_{k=1}^{n} u_{ik}^m \left\| \varphi(x_k) - \varphi(v_i) \right\|^2 \qquad (2.12)$$

Where

$$\left\| \varphi(x_k) - \varphi(v_i) \right\|^2 = k(x_k, x_k) + k(v_i, v_i) - 2k(x_k, v_i) \qquad (2.13)$$

Where $K(x,y) = \Phi(x)^T \Phi(y)$ is an inner product kernel function, adopt the Gaussian function as a kernel function, i.e., $K(x,y) = \exp(-\|x-y\|^2/\sigma^2)$, then K(x,x) = 1, according to Equation(2.13), Equation(2.12) can be rewritten as

$$J_m = 2\sum_{i=1}^{c}\sum_{k=1}^{n} u_{ik}^{m}(1 - k(x_k, v_i)) \tag{2.14}$$

Minimizing the Equation (2.14) under the constraint of $u_{ik}$, we have

$$u_{ik} = \frac{(1/(1 - k(x_k, v_i)))^{1/(m-1)}}{\sum_{j=1}^{c}(1/(1 - k(x_k, v_i)))^{1/(m-1)}} \tag{2.15}$$

$$v_i = \frac{\sum_{k=1}^{n} u_{ik}^{m} k(x_k, v_i) x_k}{\sum_{k=1}^{n} u_{ik}^{m} k(x_k, v_i)} \tag{2.16}$$

Here we just use the Gaussian kernel function for simplicity. If we use other kernel functions, there will be corresponding modifications in Equation (2.15) and Equation (2.16).

# CHAPTER 3

# GENERAL STEPS AND ACCURACY ASSESSMENT

This chapter discusses about the general steps for proposed method and accuracy assessment. The methodology for the proposed satellite image classification system for land use/land cover mapping was discussed in general steps. Accuracy of the classified satellite images based on field visit data and cluster validity measures was discussed in accuracy assessment.

## 3.1 GENERAL STEPS FOR THE PROPOSED SYSTEM

The steps involved in the proposed satellite image classification system for land use/land cover mapping are presented in Figure 3.1 which consists of the four major steps

**Step 1:** Wavelet and Contourlet Frame Based Texture Feature Extraction

**Step 2**: Feature Reduction

**Step 3**: Feature Classification

**Step 4:** Accuracy Assessment

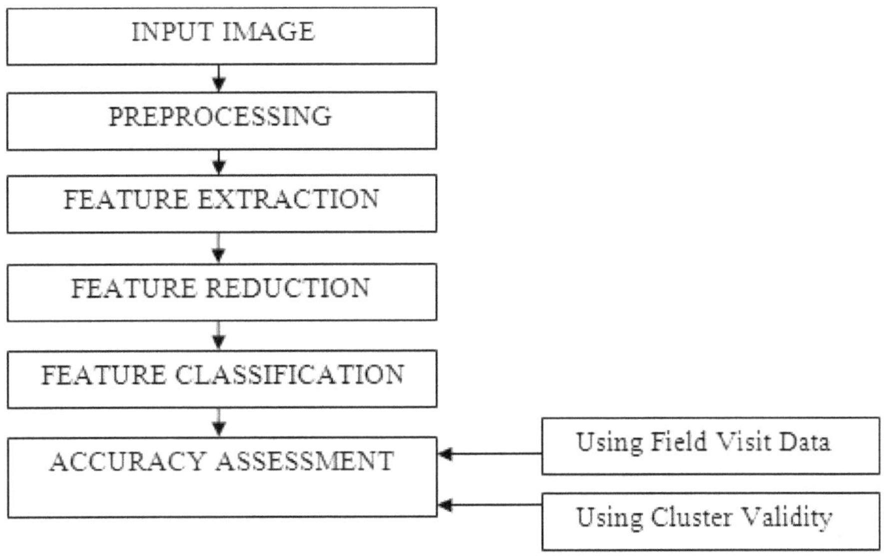


**Figure 3.1 Methodology**

## 3.2 PREPARATION OF GROUND TRUTH DATA

Field visits play an imperative role in determining Land use/Land cover features in real world. The ground truth data obtained from the various field visits were compared with the classified data from the satellite images to assess the accuracy of classification. The field visits ensured the accuracy and the success of the project. The Table 3.1 shows the latitude and longitude of different places visited.

**Table 3.1 Field Survey – Ground Control Points**

| Name of the Area | Latitude | Longitude | Elevation (Feet) | Accuracy (Feet) | Features |
|---|---|---|---|---|---|
| Alanganallur | 10°04"61.9" | 78°08"69.8" | 138 | 24 | Vegetation |
| Meenakshi amman temple | 9°91"94.4" | 78°11"94.3" | 148 | 27 | Urban |
| Vandiyur | 9°91"03.2" | 78°16"03.3" | 140 | 25 | Water |
| Alagulam tank | 9°57"25.6" | 78°07"14.4" | 138 | 24 | Water body |
| Teppakulam | 10°82"75.8" | 78°69"39.1" | 140 | 26 | Urban |
| Alagar Kovil | 10°07"41.5" | 78°21"44.1" | 128 | 21 | Hilly |
| Perungudi | 9°50"33.9" | 78°05"33.2" | 134 | 24 | Waste land |
| Mattuthavani | 9°94"41.4" | 78°15"61.5" | 127 | 22 | Urban |
| Thiruparankun dram | 9°89"00.7" | 78°05"60.0" | 125 | 22 | Hilly |
| Chinthamani | 9°53"14.8" | 78°08"37.8" | 133 | 26 | Urban |
| Melamadai | 9°55"38.9" | 78°09"06.7" | 135 | 25 | Waste land |
| Anna nagar | 9°55"04.4" | 78°08"55.3" | 140 | 29 | Urban |
| Vandiyur stop | 9°54"35.3" | 78°09"36.5" | 122 | 26 | Urban |
| Usilampatti | 9°97"00.0" | 78°80"00.3" | 126 | 24 | Waste land |
| Vaigai river | 9°54"45.3" | 78°09"20.1" | 122 | 23 | Water body |

## 3.3 ACCURACY ASSESSMENT USING GROUND TRUTH DATA

Yet another scopeful area in the field of remote sensing is the classification accuracy measurement. The method to create digital land cover classifications was far better than to quantification of their accuracy. The problem may be due to the elimination of automated land cover classification techniques. But the established fact that „A classification is not complete until its accuracy is assessed" should not be ignored.

The quantitative assessment of classification accuracy requires the field visit data or knowledge based on prior art search of the terrain that can be compared with the remote sensing based classification map. Two classification maps were used to assess the classification accuracy viz., 1) the remote sensing derived map, and 2) assumed true map. The true map based on assumption can be derived from in site investigation or based on observations made from remote sensing data with larger scale or higher resolution.

Accuracy measurements (Giles Foody 2001) were usually done on classified images to understand whether the process of classification has attained the goal. Based on unsupervised and supervised classification methods, accuracy assessments were done that spells about the quality of the data derived from the remote sensing data. Preparation of classification error matrix is the most common methods of expression of classification accuracy and at times referred to as confusion or a contingency table.

Error matrix otherwise referred as confusion matrix or contingency table compares link between the known reference data and the classification data by category by category basis. The error matrices are square with equal number of rows, columns and number of categories for which the classification accuracy needs to be measured.

Error matrix is used to verify how best a classification algorithm explained a representative subset of pixels used in the training process of a supervised or unsupervised classification. This matrix is based on the classification of sampled training set pixels and enlisting the common cover types used for training versus the pixels that are really classified into each land category by the classifier.

There are many accuracy indices in the determination of accuracy of classification like overall accuracy, producer accuracy and user accuracy. Amongst them, kappa co-efficient of agreement (Lillesand et al 2004) is the widely adopted as the standard measure of accuracy by the researchers. The classification rate can be computed using the field visit data and performance of classification algorithm can be estimated.

The different accuracy indices are defined as,

**Overall accuracy**: The overall accuracy is computed by dividing the total number of correctly classified pixels (i.e., the sum of the elements along the major diagonal) by the total number of reference pixels. The individual category accuracies are measured by dividing the number of correctly classified pixels in each category by either the total number of pixels in the corresponding row or column.

**Producer"s accuracy**: The producer accuracy is used to measure the omission error. It is determined by dividing the number of correctly classified pixels (on the major diagonal) in each category by the number of reference pixels (the column total) used for that category.

**User"s accuracy**: It is a measure of commission error and it is computed by dividing the number of correctly classified pixels in each category by the total number of pixels that were classified in that category (the row total).

**Kappa Coefficient**: The kappa coefficient is a measure of the difference between the actual agreement between reference data and an automated classifier and the chance agreement between the reference data and a random classifier. Conceptually, it can be defined as

Kappa coefficient is computed as

$$\hat{K} = \frac{N \sum_{i=1}^{r} x_{ii} - \sum_{i=1}^{r} (x_{i+} * x_{+i})}{N^2 - \sum_{i=1}^{r} (x_{i+} * x_{+i})} \tag{3.1}$$

Where,

r = number of rows in the error matrix

$x_{ii}$= number of observations in row i and column i (on the major diagonal)

$x_{i+}$= total of observations in row i (shown as marginal total to right of the matrix)

$x_{+i}$= total of observations in column i (shown as marginal total at bottom of the matrix)

N = total number of observations included in matrix

This kappa statistic serves as an indicator of the extent to which the percentage correct values of an error matrix are due to true agreement versus the chance agreement. As the reference data approaches 1 and the classified data approaches 0, K value is 1.

## 3.4 ACCURACY ASSESSMENT USING CLUSTER VALIDITY MEASURES

The process of evaluating the goodness of the resulting clusters is called the cluster validity assessment. The assessment is based on the compactness and separation of the clusters (Maria Halkidi et al., 2002a, b).The internal cluster validity measures are based on some of the metrics which is based on data set and the clustering schema. Different internal measures are used to measure the result of the cluster without any external information.

Silhouette Coefficient:

Silhouette is a measure of similarity of a feature to other feature in its own cluster and in other clusters whose value range from +1 that represents points that are distant from neighbouring clusters, 0 indicate points that are not distinct to any given cluster,-1 indicates that are assigned to wrong cluster. Lesser the silhouette value better will be the matching of clusters.

$$s(i) = \frac{b(i) - a(i)}{\max\{a(i), b(i)\}} \tag{3.2}$$

$$s(i) = \begin{cases} 1 - \dfrac{a(i)}{b(i)}, & if a(i) < b(i) \\ 0, & if a(i) = b(i) \\ \dfrac{b(i)}{a(i)} - 1, & if a(i) > b(i) \end{cases} \tag{3.3}$$

where a(i), b(i) are the two clusters.

Davis and Bouldin index:

Davis and Bouldin index is a measure of mean similarity between each cluster. Lower value of DB index represents the better cluster configuration

$$R_{ij} = \frac{s_i + s_j}{d_{ij}} \quad i \neq j \tag{3.4}$$

Where

$$d_{ij} = \left\| C_i - C_j \right\|^2 \tag{3.5}$$

$$S = \frac{1}{n_i} \sum_{j=1}^{n_i} \left\| x_j - C_i \right\|^2 \tag{3.6}$$

$$S_j = \frac{1}{n_j} \sum_{i=1}^{n_j} \left\| xi - C_j \right\|^2 \tag{3.7}$$

$$R_i = \max_{j=1,\ldots M} R_{ij} \qquad \text{where i=1,....M} \tag{3.8}$$

$$DBI = \frac{1}{M} \sum_{i=1}^{M} R_i \tag{3.9}$$

Dunns Index:

The data set has well separated and higher cluster distance with small diameter. The Dunns index is indicated as

$$D_{nc} = \min_{i=1,\ldots n_c} \left\{ \min_{j=i+1,\ldots n_c} \left\{ \frac{d(c_i, c_j)}{\max_{k=1,\ldots n_c} diam(c_k)} \right\} \right\} \tag{3.10}$$

where $d(c_i, c_j)$ is the dissimilarity function between two clusters $c_i$ and $c_j$ defined as

$$d(c_i, c_j) = \min_{x \in C_i, y \in C_j} d(x, y) \tag{3.11}$$

where diam(c) is the diameter of the cluster, which may be consider as a measure of cluster‟s dispersion. The diameter of the cluster C can be defined as follows:

$$diam(c) = \max_{x,y \in c} d(x, y) \tag{3.12}$$

Calinski - Harabasz Criterion:

Calinski - Harabasz Criterion is otherwise referred as variance ratio criterion. The well-defined clusters possessed large variance between clusters on the contrary small variance between the clusters, Higher the VRCk ratio, better the data partition.

$$CH = \frac{SSB/(M-1)}{SSW\,(N-M)} \tag{3.13}$$

Ball and Hall (BH):

The mean dispersion of a cluster is the mean of the squared distances of the points of the cluster with respect to their bar centre. The Ball-Hall index is the mean, through all the clusters of their mean dispersion and it is defined as

$$BH = \frac{SSW}{M} \tag{3.14}$$

Where SSW = Sum of Square Within the cluster

M = number of cluster

The maximum value of the successive difference is determined as the optimal number of clusters.

# CHAPTER 4

# LAND USE/LAND COVER CLASSIFICATION USING WAVELET AND CONTOURLET FRAME BASED FEATURES

This chapter analyzes the performance comparison of the wavelet, Non subsampled Contourlet, Wavelet based contourlet frame based feature extraction techniques for the classification of LISS II, LISS III, LISS IV(i) images. This chapter also discusses the performance analysis of the different kernel functions.

## 4.1 WAVELET FRAME BASED FEATURE EXTRACTION

The input images obtained from the satellite can be used to derive information on urban, vegetation, bareland, water, hilly etc. In this chapter, the performance of the scalar wavelet and contourlet frame based feature extraction techniques were analyzed. The input data was registered from the survey of Indian topographic sheets 58 K/1, in 1:50,000 scale and rest four 58 K/1 SW, SE, NW, NE in 1:25,000 scale are used as reference data for ground control points (GCP) collection and validation. The standard errors are below 0.5 pixels along X and Y directions were maintained. A sub image size of 400 x 400 pixels is extracted from the original scale.

Contourlet transform

Contourlet transform is a subsampled transform. The input image shown here for processing is LISS - II red band Madurai imagery consists of size 400 × 400. From the first level decomposition of the red band image, low and high frequency components are obtained. The low frequency consists of image size 200 × 200. The high pass sub band was further applied to directional filter banks to provide more detailed information about the directional components. For n = 4 the high pass subband image is further divided in to 16 sub bands each with size 50× 200 or 200 × 50 columns as shown in Figure 4.2 a. The same process is applied to the remaining bands of LISS II, LISS III and LISS IV images. The process was repeated up to maximum level of decomposition (here n = 4). Decomposition at level 2 for the Madurai red band imagery is shown in Figure 4.2 b. Due to subsampling problem principal component analysis based feature reduction technique is not able to convert the features in to original image size.

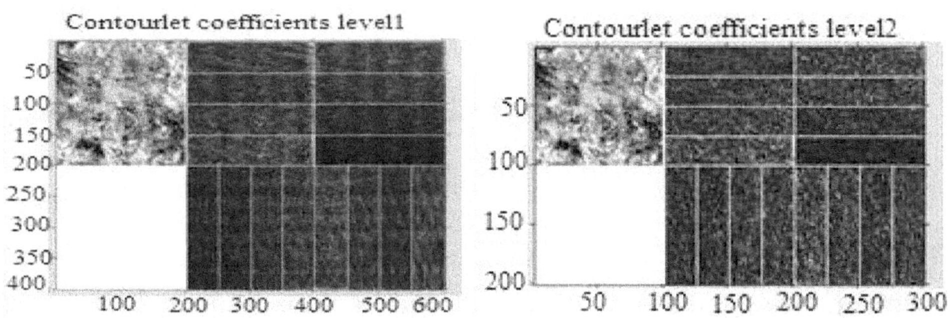


(a) (b)

**Figure 4.1 Decomposed LISS – II image after to Contourlet transform (a) Level-1 decomposition (b) Level-2 decomposition**

## 4.2 NONSUBSAMPLED CONTOURLET FRAME BASED FEATURE EXTRACTION

The disadvantage of wavelet frame transform is the non availability of directional components. The contourlet transform is a subsampled transform which gives more detail components of high frequency images. Due to the sub sampling problem, an efficient and flexible transformation such as Non subsampled contourlet transform (NSCT) was used where redundancy is not a major issue (e.g., denoising). Nonsubsampled contourlet is based on the theory of contourlet transform is a flexible multiscale, multidirection, and shift-invariant image analysis method and it was able to sufficiently capture the geometrical details of the source image. The operation of NSCT was similar to contourlet but the image will not be subsampled as shown in Figure 4.3 a & b.

The NSCT is constructed by combining two parts, i.e., the Non subsampled pyramidal filter bank (NSPFB) and Nonsubsampled directional filter bank (NSDFB). The former part ensured the multiscale property by employing two-channel non subsampled filter banks. At each NSPFB decomposition stage, a low-pass subband, together with a high-pass one, can be produced.

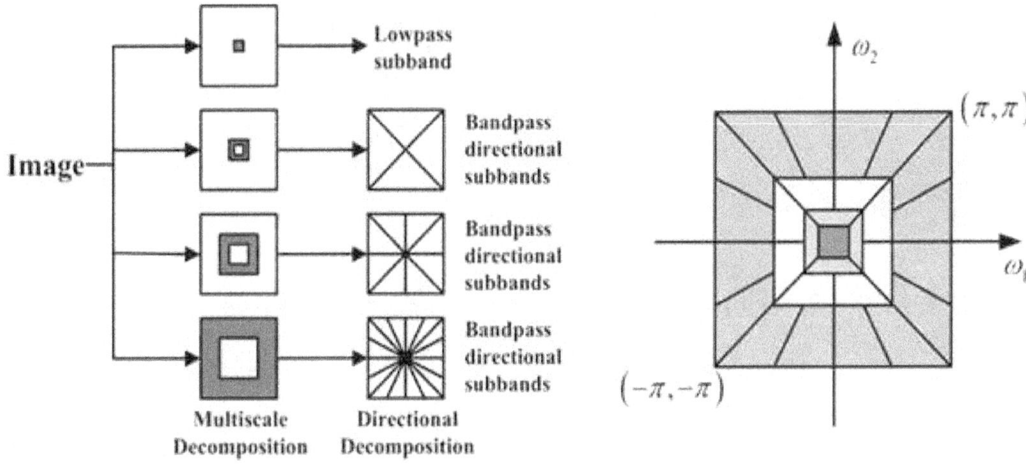


a) b)

**Figure 4.2 NSCT a) Process of NSCT b) Directional splitting**

The subsequent NSPFB decomposition stages iteratively decomposed the low-pass sub band available to capture the singularities in the image. Since the filter banks are non subsampled, all the obtained low-pass and high-pass subbands have same size as that of source image. The NSDFB, constructed by combining the two-channel Non subsampled directional filter banks. The NSDFB allowed the direction decomposition with $l$ levels in high-pass subbands from NSPFB at each scale and produces $2^l$ directional sub bands with the same size as the source image. Thus, the NSDFB endows the NSCT with the multidirectional property.

**Figure 4.3 Directional components of high pass sub band of LISS II image**

NSCT is redundant transform in which the original image size gets maintained after decomposition without reduction in the original pixel size. The operation of NSCT is similar to contourlet but the image would not be subsampled. The directional filter applied to high pass is in level four, 16-directional information of the LISS II red band image as shown in Figure 4.4. The low pass image was then applied for the next level decomposition to get the more detailed information. The process is repeated up to the maximum level of decomposition (here n = 4). The same process was applied to the remaining bands of LISS II, LISS III and LISS IV (i) imagery.

## 4.3 WAVELET AND CONTOURLET FRAME BASED FEATURE EXTRACTION

The Wavelet Based Contourlet Transform (WBCT) which is based on the theory of contourlet transform is a flexible multi scale, multiresolution, multidirection and shift-invariant image analysis method, which is able to sufficiently capture the geometrical details of the source image. The WBCT was constructed by combining two parts, i.e., Stationary Wavelet Transform (SWT) and Non Subsampled Directional Filter Bank (NSDFB). At each decomposition SWT was applied to produce approximation and detailed components. Since the filter banks are nonsubsampled, all obtained low-pass and high-pass subbands have the same size of the source image. The NSDFB, constructed by combining the directional filter banks devised by Bamberger and Smith is also two-channel nonsubsampled filter banks. The NSDFB allows the direction decomposition with F stages in detailed subbands from SWT at each scale and produces $2^r$directional subbands with the same size as the source image. Thus, the NSDFB endows WBCT with multidirectional property.

In the WBCT shown in Figure 4.5, Two-dimensional separable wavelet transform is applied on the LISS II red band input image by dividing in to four sub bands (LL, LH, HL, and HH). From this the last three high frequency sub bands were further divided by the directional filter banks as shown in Figure 4.6. High frequency sub bands are then segmented in to several directions. The low pass sub band was applied to the next stage to get more detailed information. The wavelet based contourlet frame transform is used for decomposition. The process was repeated up to the maximum level of decomposition (here n = 4). The same process was applied to the remaining bands of the input images.

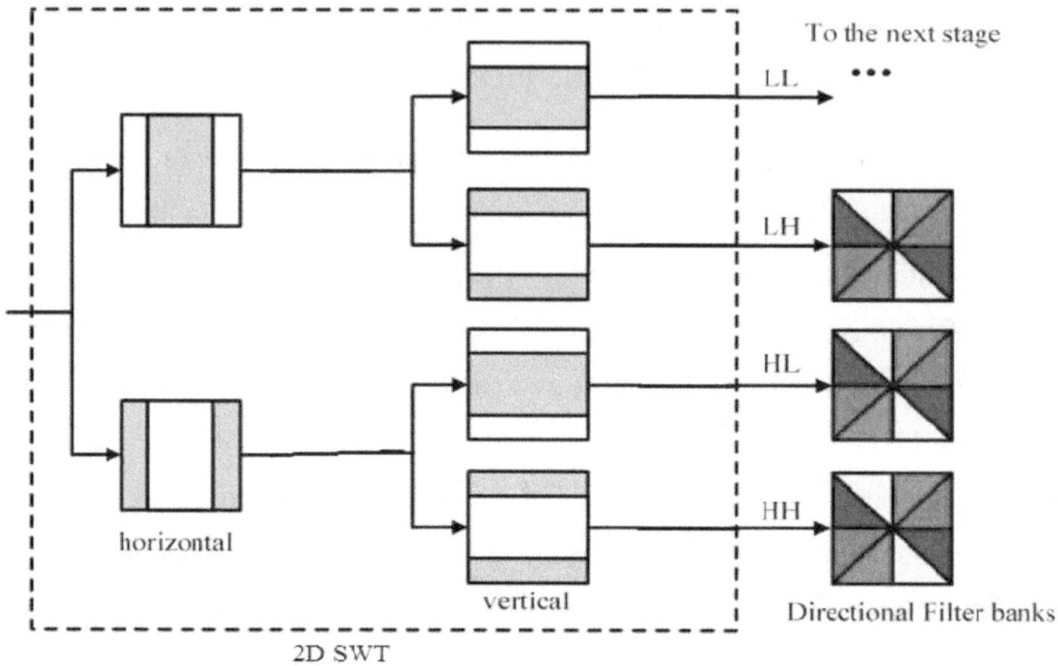


**Figure 4.4 Wavelet Based Contourlet transform**

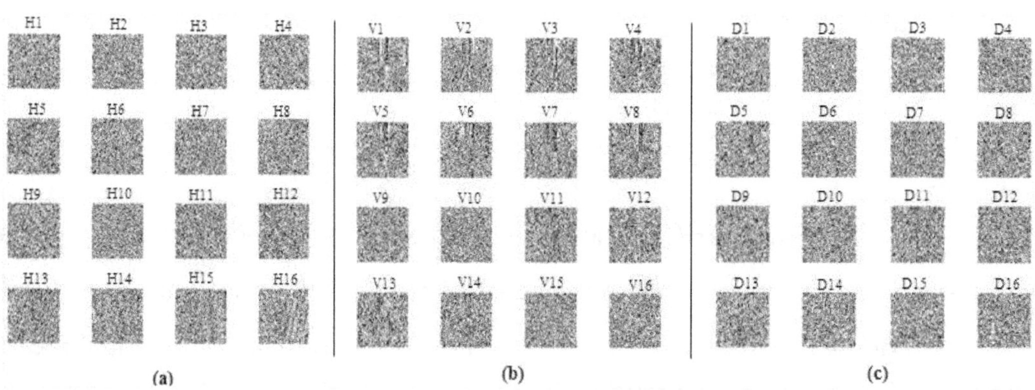


**Figure 4.5 Directional coefficients of LISS - II image (a) LH (b) HL (c) HH**

The output from the texture feature extraction is a set of images. These images are the feature images that will form the basis for the classification. They are used to form feature vectors, where each feature image corresponds to one element in the feature vectors. Classification was performed based on the feature vectors.

## 4.4 PCA BASED FEATURE REDUCTION

PCA has been applied to feature sets comprising of different bands of input images. The n number of features for an image of size MxN. Feature vector x of the image is of dimension MN x n where the each column represents the features (xk) of the respective pixel in the image.

The mean vector of the population is defined as

$$m_x = \frac{1}{M}\sum_{k=1}^{M} x_k \tag{4.1}$$

The covariance matrix of the population is defined as

$$C_x = E(x_k x_k^T) - m_x m_x^T \tag{4.2}$$

where k = 1, 2, . . . M

For the covariance matrix $C_x$ n orthonormal eigen vectors are calculated. The output Eigen channels produced by the principal component transformation has a large dynamic range, especially the first few layers which pack most of the information.

## 4.5 FEATURE CLASSIFICATION AND MAPPING USING GAUSSIAN KERNELS

The feature extracted image should be processed to discriminate between the classifications accurately. The feature vector obtained by feature extraction was sorted out into classification using Gaussian kernel. Different kernel functions were used to analyze the performance of the classification. The classification accuracy tends to decrease for other kernel functions as shown in Table 4.1.

**Table 4.1 Accuracy Assessment Using Different Kernel functions**

| Techniques used | Over all Accuracy | Kappa Coefficient |
|---|---|---|
| Linear Kernel | 84.03 | 0.7695 |
| Polynomial Kernel | 84.27 | 0.78 |
| Log Kernel | 84.87 | 0.7826 |
| Gaussian Kernel | 86.13 | 0.8002 |

Among the different kernel functions used, Gaussian kernel outperformed well and it resulted in better accuracy results. The Gaussian kernel is defined as

$$k(x,y) = 1 - \exp\left( \frac{-\|x-y\|^2}{\sigma^2} \right) \tag{4.3}$$

The main function of the kernel is to allow linear evaluation of feature vector in to higher dimensional feature space that resulted in non linear clusters of data samples present in the input space. The higher dimensional features space was generated by a mapping function applied on the feature extracted images.

The aim of image classification is to automatically categorize all features in an image into land cover classes or themes. The advantage of fuzzy clustering technique over the indigenous clustering techniques is that the former assigns different degrees of membership to each pixel. The soft clustering needs to be compulsorily converted into hard clustering for cluster validity measures. For this conversion, a pixel with high membership value was assigned to the corresponding cluster. The algorithm should be iteratively optimized to find out fair partition of clusters.

## 4.6 EXPERIMENTAL RESULTS AND DISCUSSION

Any classification technique is incomplete until its accuracy is assessed. Several accuracy indices (Giles Foody., 2001) such as overall accuracy, producer accuracy, user accuracy were used to determine the accuracy of classification by several workers. Kappa coefficient (Lillesand, *et al.,* 2004) of agreement was the standard means of measurement of accuracy of classification in remote sensing. Using the field visit data the classification rate was computed and performances of classification algorithms were analyzed. Using the various internal cluster validity measures, the computed classification rates for different feature extraction techniques were analyzed.

Results using LISS II image

Experimental study was carried out to select the best feature extraction method for the classification of LISS II Madurai image. The Classified input image LISS II using Wavelet, NSCT, and WBCT were shown in Figure 4.6. The confusion matrices obtained from the classification results using wavelet transform, NSCT, WBCT are shown in Tables 4.2- 4.4 respectively.

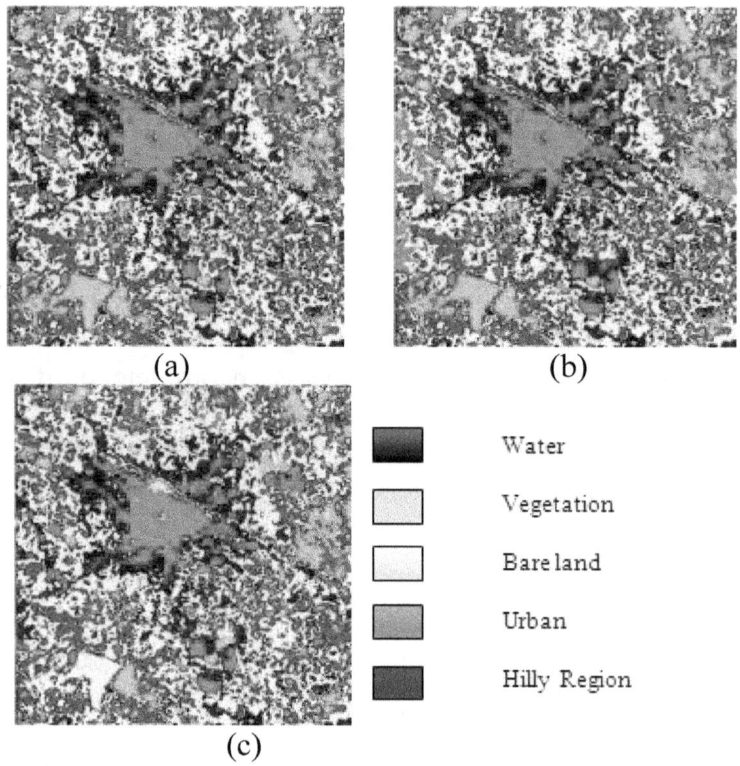


**Figure 4.6 Classified output of LISS II image using (a) Wavelet, (b) NSCT, (c) WBCT**

**Table 4.2 Confusion Matrix using Wavelet transform for LISS II image**

| **LISSII** | Urban | Vegetation | Waste land | Hilly | Water | Total row |
|---|---|---|---|---|---|---|
| Urban | 140 | 10 | 10 | 10 | 5 | 175 |
| Vegetation | 10 | 135 | 5 | 5 | 5 | 160 |
| Waste land | 5 | 5 | 122 | 5 | 5 | 142 |
| Hilly | 4 | 3 | 3 | 88 | 3 | 101 |
| Water | 5 | 5 | 4 | 3 | 105 | 122 |
| Total column | 164 | 158 | 144 | 111 | 123 | 700 |

**Table 4.3 Confusion Matrix using NSCT for LISS II image**

| **LISSII** | Urban | Vegetation | Waste land | Hilly | Water | Total row |
|---|---|---|---|---|---|---|
| Urban | 141 | 10 | 9 | 10 | 5 | 175 |
| Vegetation | 10 | 137 | 4 | 4 | 5 | 160 |
| Waste land | 5 | 4 | 123 | 5 | 5 | 142 |
| Hilly | 2 | 3 | 3 | 90 | 3 | 101 |
| Water | 5 | 5 | 3 | 3 | 106 | 122 |
| Total column | 163 | 159 | 142 | 112 | 124 | 700 |

**Table 4.4 Confusion Matrix using WBCT for LISS II image**

| **LISS II** | Urban | Vegetation | Waste land | Hilly | Water | Total row |
|---|---|---|---|---|---|---|
| Urban | 143 | 9 | 9 | 9 | 5 | 175 |
| Vegetation | 9 | 138 | 4 | 4 | 5 | 160 |
| Waste land | 4 | 4 | 125 | 4 | 5 | 142 |
| Hilly | 2 | 3 | 2 | 91 | 3 | 101 |
| Water | 5 | 3 | 3 | 3 | 108 | 122 |
| Total column | 163 | 157 | 143 | 111 | 126 | 700 |

**Table 4.5 Results for LISS II image using Wavelet, NSCT, WBCT**

| **LISS II image** | **Accuracy indices** | | | |
|---|---|---|---|---|
| | **User Accuracy** | **Producer Accuracy** | **Overall Accuracy** | **Kappa** |
| Wavelet | 81.26 | 78.94 | 82.0 | 0.8144 |
| NSCT | 82.06 | 79.11 | 84.64 | 0.8368 |
| WBCT | 83.3 | 80.3 | 86.80 | 0.8785 |

The quantitative results obtained with the classified map, shown in Tables 4.2- 4.4 are summarized in the Table 4.5. By observing Table 4.5, it is evident that wavelet based contourlet transform gave better accuracy results.

Results using LISS III image

Experimental study was carried out to select the best feature extraction method for the classification of LISS III Madurai images using wavelet, NSCT, WBCT. The Classified input images LISS III using Wavelet, NSCT, WBCT were shown in Figure 4.7. The confusion matrices obtained from the classification results using wavelet, NSCT and WBCT were shown in Tables 4.6-4.8 respectively.

(c)

**Figure 4.7 Classified output of LISS III image using (a) Wavelet, (b) NSCT, (c) WBCT**

**Table 4.6 Confusion Matrix using Wavelet for LISS III image**

| LISSIII | Urban | Vegetation | Waste land | Hilly | Water | Total row |
|---|---|---|---|---|---|---|
| Urban | 139 | 10 | 11 | 10 | 5 | 175 |
| Vegetation | 10 | 136 | 4 | 5 | 5 | 160 |
| Waste land | 5 | 6 | 121 | 5 | 5 | 142 |
| Hilly | 4 | 3 | 3 | 89 | 2 | 101 |
| Water | 5 | 5 | 5 | 3 | 104 | 122 |
| Total column | 163 | 160 | 144 | 112 | 121 | 700 |

**Table 4.7 Confusion Matrix using NSCT for LISS III image**

| LISSIII | Urban | Vegetation | Waste land | Hilly | Water | Total row |
|---|---|---|---|---|---|---|
| Urban | 141 | 10 | 9 | 10 | 5 | 175 |
| Vegetation | 10 | 138 | 4 | 3 | 5 | 160 |
| Waste land | 5 | 5 | 122 | 5 | 5 | 142 |
| Hilly | 4 | 2 | 2 | 91 | 2 | 101 |
| Water | 5 | 4 | 5 | 3 | 105 | 122 |
| Total column | 165 | 159 | 142 | 112 | 122 | 700 |

**Table 4.8 Confusion Matrix using WBCT for LISS III image**

| LISS III | Urban | Vegetation | Waste land | Hilly | Water | Total row |
|---|---|---|---|---|---|---|
| Urban | 142 | 9 | 9 | 10 | 5 | 175 |
| Vegetation | 9 | 139 | 4 | 3 | 5 | 160 |
| Waste land | 4 | 4 | 124 | 5 | 5 | 142 |
| Hilly | 3 | 2 | 2 | 92 | 2 | 101 |
| Water | 4 | 4 | 4 | 3 | 107 | 122 |
| Total column | 162 | 158 | 143 | 113 | 124 | 700 |

**Table 4.9 Results for LISS III image using Wavelet, NSCT, WBCT**

| LISS III image | Accuracy indices | | | |
|---|---|---|---|---|
| | User Accuracy | Producer Accuracy | Overall Accuracy | Kappa |
| Wavelet | 82.4 | 80.6 | 84.9 | 0.844 |
| NSCT | 83.0 | 81.2 | 85.8 | 0.854 |
| WBCT | 84.8 | 83.4 | 86.2 | 0.871 |

The quantitative results obtained with the classified map, shown in Tables 4.6-4.8 are summarized in the Table 4.9. By observing Table 4.9, it is evident that wavelet based contourlet transform gives better accuracy results for LISS III image.

Results using LISS IV (i) image

Experimental study was carried out to select the best feature extraction method for the classification of LISS IV(i) Madurai image. The Classified input images LISS IV (i) using Wavelet, NSCT, WBCT were shown in Figure 4.8. The confusion matrices obtained from the classification results using Wavelet, NSCT, and WBCT were shown in Tables 4.10- 4.12 respectively.

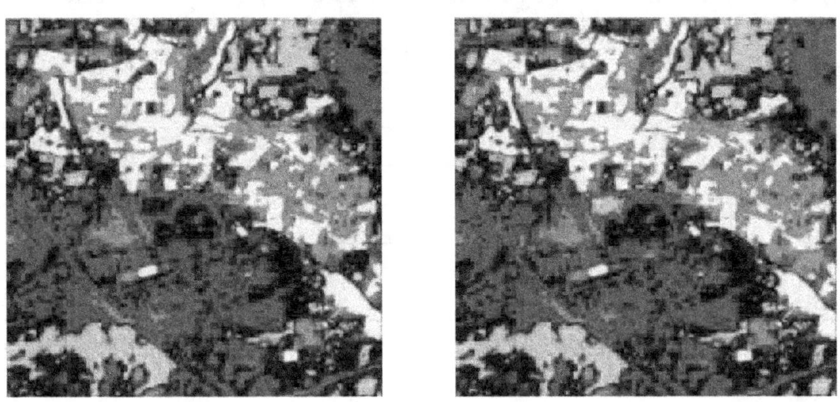

(a) (b)

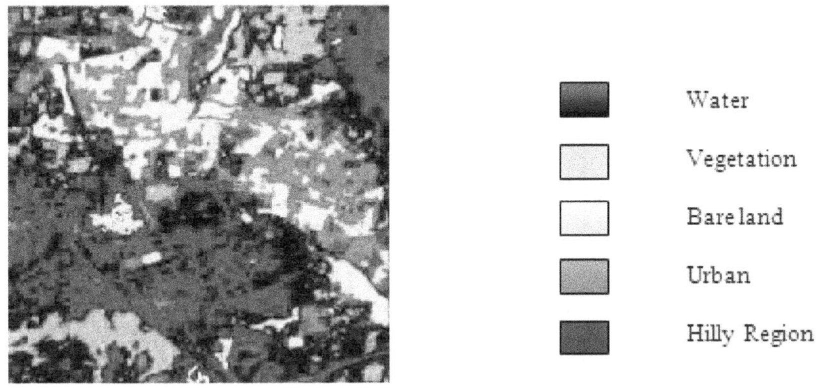


(c)

**Figure 4.8 Classified output of LISS IV (i) image using (a) Wavelet, (b) NSCT, (c) WBCT**

**Table 4.10 Confusion Matrix using Wavelet for LISS IV (i) image**

| **LISS IV(i)** | Urban | Vegetation | Waste land | Hilly | Water | Total row |
|---|---|---|---|---|---|---|
| Urban | 141 | 10 | 9 | 10 | 5 | 175 |
| Vegetation | 10 | 135 | 5 | 5 | 5 | 160 |
| Waste land | 5 | 4 | 123 | 5 | 5 | 142 |
| Hilly | 4 | 3 | 3 | 88 | 3 | 101 |
| Water | 5 | 5 | 3 | 3 | 106 | 122 |
| Total column | 165 | 157 | 143 | 111 | 124 | 700 |

**Table 4.11 Confusion Matrix using NSCT for LISS IV (i) image**

| **LISS IV(i)** | Urban | Vegetation | Waste land | Hilly | Water | Total row |
|---|---|---|---|---|---|---|
| Urban | 142 | 10 | 9 | 9 | 5 | 175 |
| Vegetation | 8 | 137 | 5 | 5 | 5 | 160 |
| Waste land | 5 | 4 | 124 | 5 | 4 | 142 |
| Hilly | 3 | 2 | 3 | 90 | 3 | 101 |
| Water | 5 | 4 | 3 | 3 | 107 | 122 |
| Total column | 163 | 157 | 144 | 112 | 124 | 700 |

**Table 4.12 Confusion Matrix using WBCT for LISS IV (i) image**

| **LISS IV(i)** | Urban | Vegetation | Waste land | Hilly | Water | Total row |
|---|---|---|---|---|---|---|
| Urban | 144 | 9 | 8 | 9 | 5 | 175 |
| Vegetation | 7 | 138 | 5 | 5 | 5 | 160 |
| Waste land | 5 | 4 | 126 | 4 | 3 | 142 |
| Hilly | 3 | 2 | 2 | 91 | 3 | 101 |
| Water | 4 | 4 | 3 | 2 | 109 | 122 |
| Total column | 163 | 157 | 144 | 111 | 125 | 700 |

**Table 4.13 Results for LISS II LISS III and LISS IV (i) image for Wavelet Based Contourlet transform**

| **LISS IV(i) image** | **Accuracy indices** | | | |
|---|---|---|---|---|
| | User Accuracy | Producer Accuracy | Overall Accuracy | Kappa |
| Wavelet | 82.9 | 81.2 | 83.90 | 0.846 |
| NSCT | 84.1 | 83.5 | 86.2 | 0.865 |
| WBCT | 88.88 | 85.4 | 87.2 | 0.894 |

The quantitative results obtained with the classified map are shown in Tables 4.10- 4.12 are summarized in the Table 4.13. By observing Table 4.13 Wavelet based contourlet transform gave better accuracy results for LISS IV (i) image.

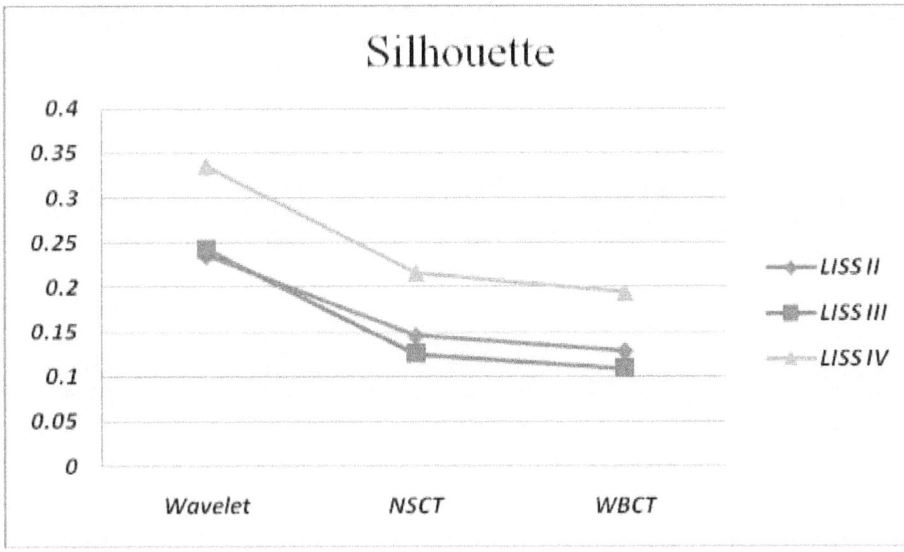


**Figure 4.9 Cluster Validity index using Silhouette value**

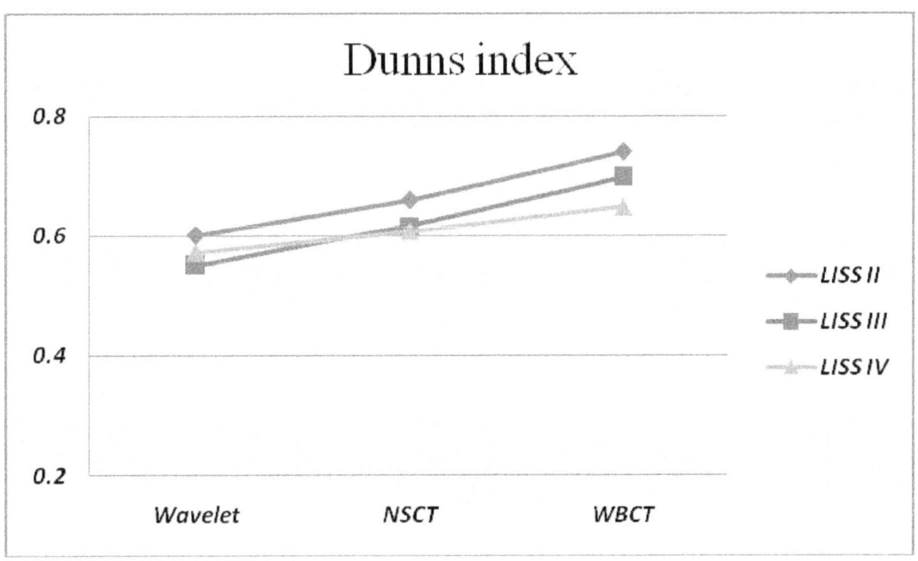


**Figure 4.10 Cluster Validity index using Dunns index**

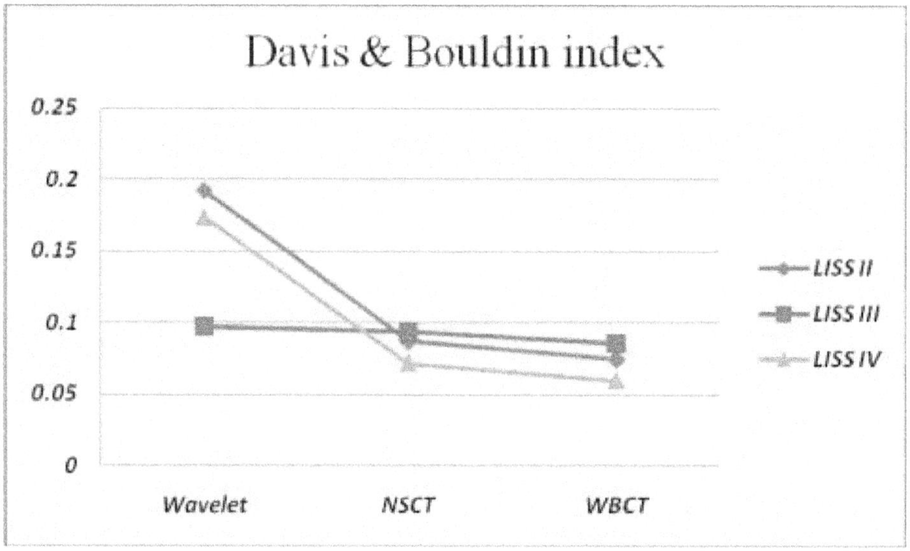


**Figure 4.11 Cluster Validity measures using Davis and Bouldin index**

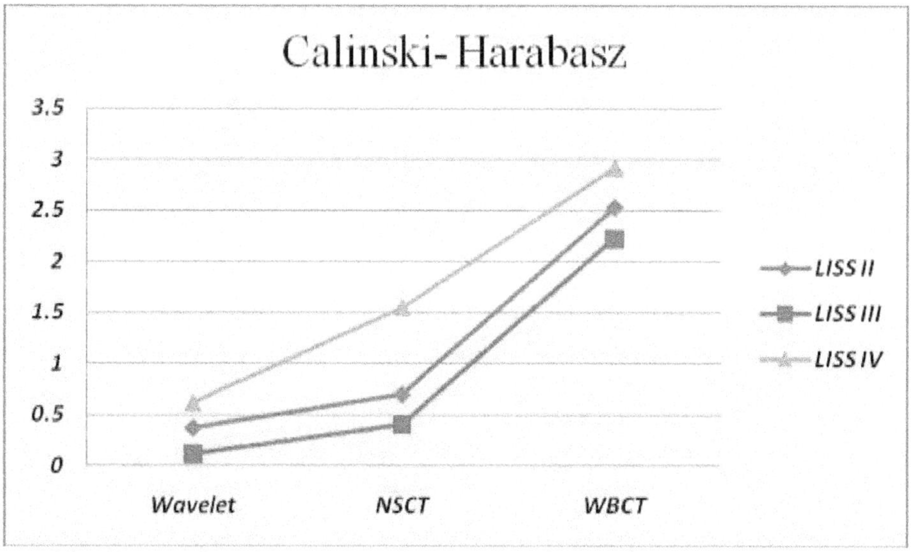


**Figure 4.12 Cluster Validity measures using Calinski Harabasz**

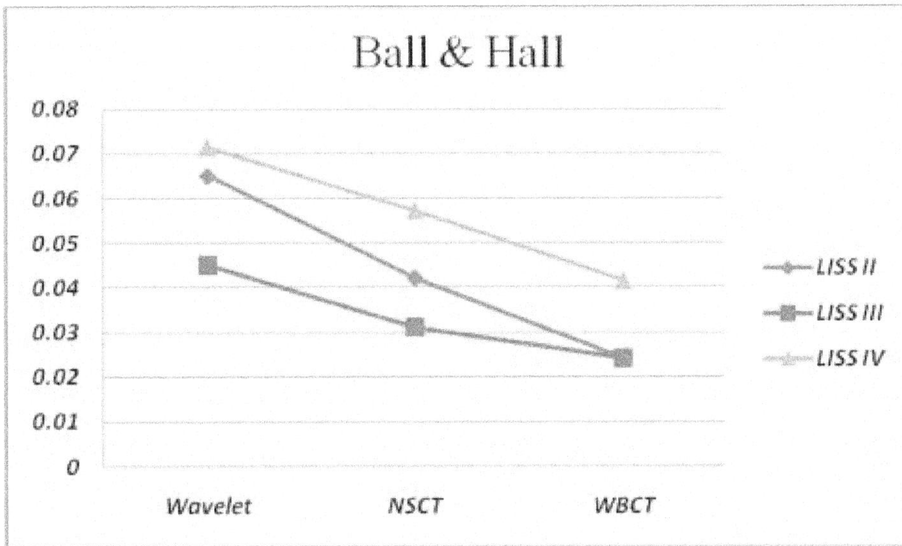


**Figure 4.13 Cluster Validity index using Ball and Hall**

It was evident from the graph shown in Figure 4.9- 4.13 the cluster validity measures for the classified LISS II, LISS III and LISS IV(i) images, Wavelet based contourlet transform provided better cluster validity results.

# CHAPTER 5

# LAND USE/LAND COVER MAPPING USING MULTIWAVELET FRAME BASED FEATURES

This chapter analyzes the performance of different scalar wavelets and multi wavelets using LISS IV (ii) image. The scalar wavelets used here for processing the satellite images includes Daubechies, Coiflet, Symlet, Bio orthogonal, Meyer and the Multi wavelets used here for processing includes GHM and Chui-Lian multiwavelets.

## 5.1 GHM & CL MULTIWAVELETS

The polynomial Multiwavelets are first constructed by Alpert, and used them as basis for some operators. After that Geronimo, Hardin and Massopust had done the construction of multi scaling function with the help of fractal interpolation.

For multiplicity of 2, equation (5.1) represents the relation of scaling functions _1(t) and _2(t) with low pass filter coefficients and similarly equation (5.2) represents the relation of wavelet functions _1(t) and _2(t) with high pass filter coefficients.

$$\left\{ \phi(t) = \begin{bmatrix} \phi_1(t) \\ \phi_2(t) \end{bmatrix} = H_0\,\phi(2t) + H_1\,\phi(2t-1) + H_2\,\phi(2t-2) + H_3\,\phi(2t-3) \right\} \quad (5.1)$$

$$\left\{ \varphi(t) = \begin{bmatrix} \varphi_1(t) \\ \varphi_2(t) \end{bmatrix} = G_0\,\phi(2t) + G_1\,\phi(2t-1) + G_2\,\phi(2t-2) + G_3\,\phi(2t-3) \right\} \quad (5.2)$$

Low pass filter coefficients $H_k$"s and high pass filter coefficients $G_k$"s for GHM are listed below

$$H_0 = \begin{bmatrix} 3/5 & 4\sqrt{2}/5 \\ -1/10\sqrt{2} & -3/10 \end{bmatrix} \qquad H_1 = \begin{bmatrix} 3/10 & 0 \\ 9\sqrt{2}/40 & 1/2 \end{bmatrix} \tag{5.3}$$

$$H_2 = \begin{bmatrix} 0 & 0 \\ 9\sqrt{2}/40 & -3/20 \end{bmatrix} \qquad H_3 = \begin{bmatrix} 0 & 0 \\ -\sqrt{2}/40 & 0 \end{bmatrix} \tag{5.4}$$

$$G_0 = \begin{bmatrix} 3/10 & 2\sqrt{2}/5 \\ -\sqrt{2}/40 & -3/20 \end{bmatrix} \qquad G_1 = \begin{bmatrix} 3/10 & 2\sqrt{2}/5 \\ -\sqrt{2}/40 & -3/20 \end{bmatrix} \tag{5.5}$$

$$G_2 = \begin{bmatrix} 3/10 & 2\sqrt{2}/5 \\ -\sqrt{2}/40 & -3/20 \end{bmatrix} \qquad G_3 = \begin{bmatrix} 3/10 & 2\sqrt{2}/5 \\ -2/40 & -3/20 \end{bmatrix} \tag{5.6}$$

GHM multiwavelets possess important properties like its scaling functions are symmetric with short support [0, 1] and [0, 2]. Scaling functions are orthogonal and multiwavelet functions are symmetric/anti symmetric pair. This multi wavelet provides second order approximation.

Another interesting multiwavelet CL of multiplicity r posses the low pass filter coefficients $H_k$'s and high pass filter coefficients $G_k$'s listed below as equations

$$H_0 = \begin{bmatrix} 1/4 & 1/4 \\ -\sqrt{7/8} & -\sqrt{7/8} \end{bmatrix} \qquad H_1 = \begin{bmatrix} 1/2 & 0 \\ 0 & 1/4 \end{bmatrix} \qquad H_2 = \begin{bmatrix} 1/4 & -14 \\ -\sqrt{7/8} & -\sqrt{7/8} \end{bmatrix} \tag{5.7}$$

$$G_0 = \begin{bmatrix} -1/4 & -1/4 \\ 1/8 & 1/8 \end{bmatrix} \qquad G_1 = \begin{bmatrix} 1/2 & 0 \\ 0 & \sqrt{7/20} \end{bmatrix} \qquad G_2 = \begin{bmatrix} -1/4 & 1/4 \\ -1/8 & 1/8 \end{bmatrix} \tag{5.8}$$

The Chui-Lian multiwavelet also has some important properties like both of its scaling functions have short support of [0, 2]. Wavelet functions and scaling functions are symmetric and anti symmetric orthonormal pairs. The vital properties cannot be fulfilled at a time in scalar wavelets. The filter coefficients used in multiwavelet involves matrices that provide more degree of freedom in designing and applications and hence yields better performance unlike scalar wavelets. The scaling and wavelet functions for GHM was represented graphically as shown in Figure 5.1.

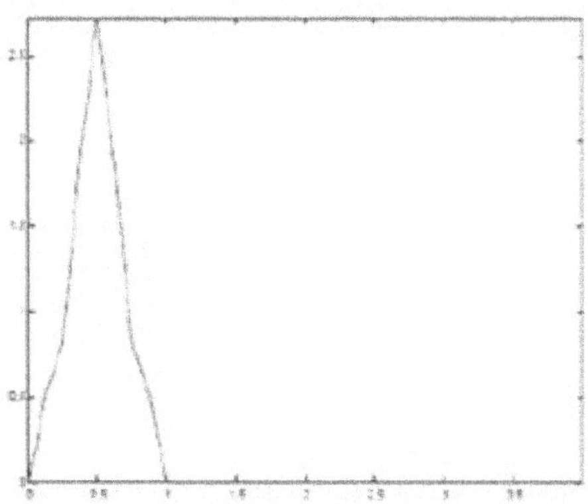

**GHM scaling function #1**

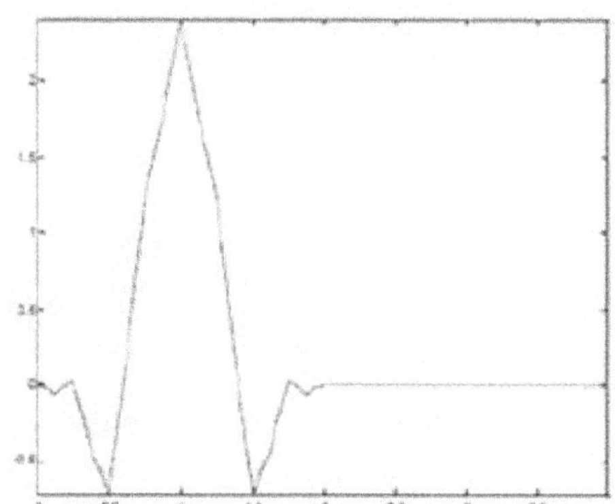

**GHM scaling function #2**

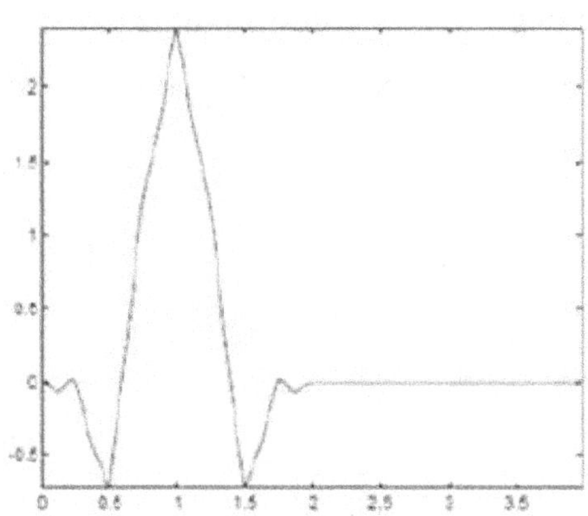

**GHM wavelet function #1**

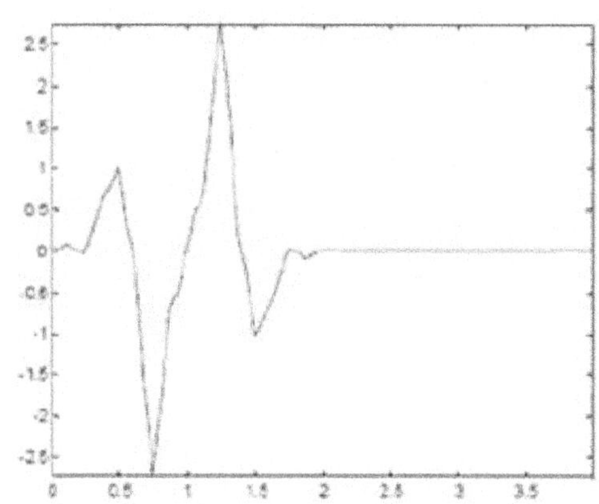

**GHM wavelet function #2**

**Figure 5.1 a)Scaling functions _1(t) and _2(t) b)wavelet functions _1 (t) and _2 (t) for GHM Multiwavelet**

Graphical representation of scaling and wavelet functions for CL Multiwavelet is given in Figure5.2.

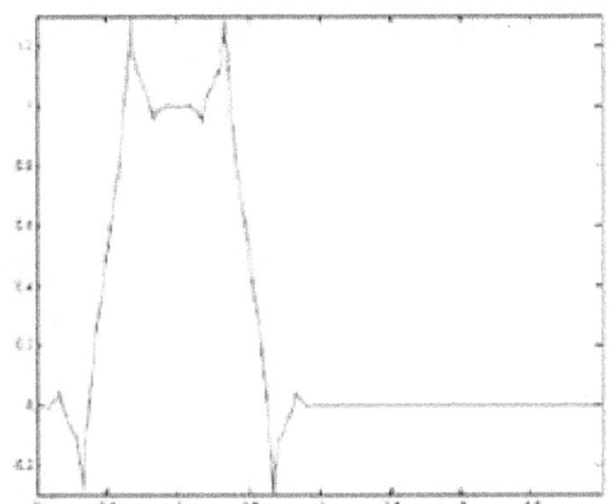

**Chui- Lian scaling function #1**

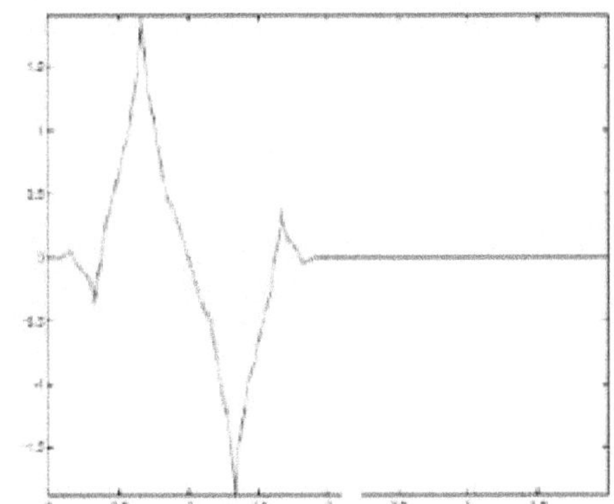

**Chui- Lian scaling function #2**

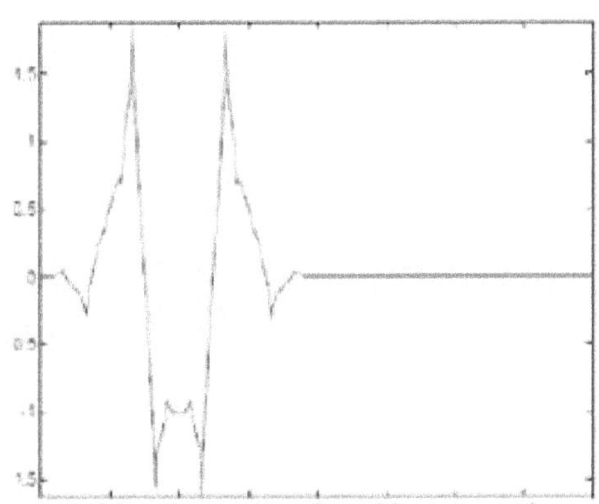

**Chui- Lian wavelet function #1**

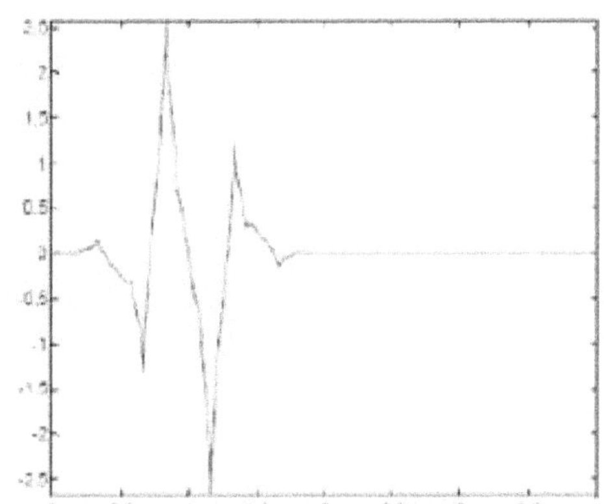

**Chui- Lian wavelet function #2**

**Figure5.2 a)Scaling functions _1(t)and _2(t) b)Wavelet functions _1 (t) and _2 (t) for CL Multiwavelet**

## 5.2 MULTIWAVELET DECOMPOSITION

The decomposition procedure and structure for multiwavelet decomposition differ from scalar wavelet decomposition. For single level decomposition in scalar wavelets, the 2D image was replaced with four subbands whereas for multiwavelets it provided 16 sub bands for single level decomposition. Multiwavelets (Pooneh Bagheri Zadeh et al. 2011) possess two scaling functions and two wavelet functions (Ivan W. Selesnick 1998) in each dimension. Using the idea of separable decomposition along each dimension of a 2D image, the preprocessing is carried out; first along rows by taking the tensor product of the prefilter with 2D image followed by multiwavelet decomposition along rows as per the multiwavelet decomposition (Shutao, Li et al. 2003) algorithm detailed in following subsection. The same process of prefiltering and first level vector valued decomposition was then performed on the resulting transformed image, but now along the columns. This completes one level of decomposition of multiwavelet transform which is shown in the Figure 5.3.

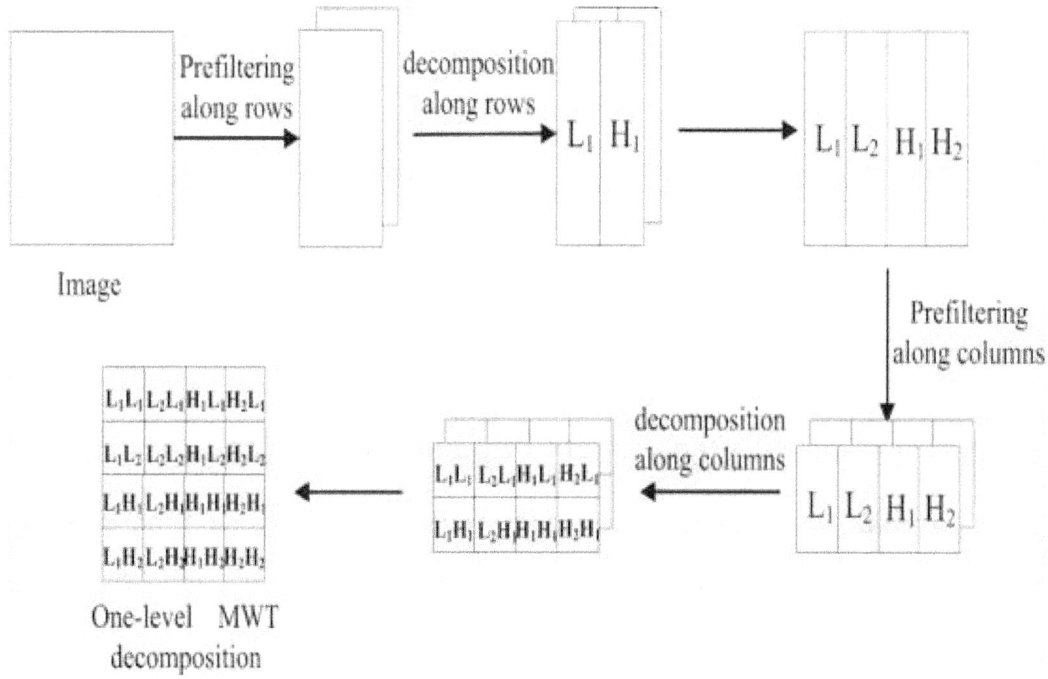


**Figure 5.3 Single level Decomposition of Multiwavelet transform**

The subband structure obtained by multiwavelet decomposition was different from a scalar wavelet due to its multichannel nature. The multiwavelets used here have two channels, so there will be two sets of scaling coefficients and two sets of multiwavelet coefficients. During single level scalar wavelet decomposition, 2D image was replaced with four blocks corresponding to the subbands representing either low pass or high pass filtering in each direction. The multiwavelet decomposition subband structure for a single level decomposition was illustrated in Figure 5.4 respectively. The L and H labels have subscripts denoting the channel to which the data correspond. The four 2x2 subbands are correspondingly denoted as $L_iL_j$, $L_iH_j$, $H_iL_j$, $H_iH_j$ with i, j=1,2.

Since the multiple iterations over the low pass data are desired, the scaling coefficients for the two channels are stored together and similarly the wavelet coefficients for the two channels are also stored together. For example, the subband labeled $L_2H_1$ corresponds to data from first channel high pass filter in the horizontal direction (row wise) and the second channel low pass filter in the vertical direction (column wise). Likewise, the subband labeled $H_1L_2$ corresponds to data from second channel low pass filtered in horizontal direction (row wise) and first channel high pass filter in the vertical direction (column wise).

| | | | |
|---|---|---|---|
| $L_1L_1$ | $L_1L_2$ | $L_1H_1$ | $L_1H_2$ |
| $L_2L_1$ | $L_2L_2$ | $L_2H_1$ | $L_2H_2$ |
| $H_1L_1$ | $H_1L_2$ | $H_1H_1$ | $H_1H_2$ |
| $H_2L_1$ | $H_2L_2$ | $H_2H_1$ | $H_2H_2$ |

**Figure 5.4 Single Level Multiwavelet Decomposition- Subband Structure**

Figure 5.4 shows at the end of the first level 2D multiwavelet decomposition, 16 intermediate image sub bands are formed. The four sub bands in the upper left corner of the current intermediate image belong to the approximate version of the original image, while the other subbands constitute the detail version of the original image in different orientations. In case of scalar wavelet decomposition, a single quarter sized low pass sub band (LL) was formed from the original larger sub band, which was fully used for the next level of decomposition.

Stationary Multiwavelet Transform

Due to the advantages of multiwavelet transformation, in this research stationary multiwavelet transform (Ali Zifan et al. 2010) was used for feature extraction which is translation invariance. Stationary scalar wavelet transform gave out an algorithm to overcome the lack of translation invariance, where the low pass and high pass filters are interpolated with zeros *i.e.,* instead of down sampling process up sampling was performed. Similarly for stationary multiwavelet transform it was interpolated with rxr zero matrix because the coefficients of filter is a matrix. The first level approximation and detail coefficients are of same size as that of original image data.

## 5.3 EXPERIMENTAL RESULTS AND DISCUSSION

The experimental study was carried out for the LISS IV (ii) Madurai image to extract the features for classification. To extract features, the given input image size is 512*512, the input image has five classes of areas- vegetation, urban, bare land, water body and hilly region. Prefiltering along the rows was performed, in this research repeated row pre-processing was implemented which is equivalent to over sampling, as the single row input was converted to two input rows. Similarly pre filtering along column was performed, as the result the size of the input image got doubled i.e., the input image of size 512*512 is being converted to 1024*1024, as it is the over sampling method. The extracted feature was converted to feature vector and the reduced feature set was obtained using principal component analysis method and the image was classified using Gaussian kernel fuzzy classifier. The classified image of LISS IV (ii) image using different scalar and multiwavelets was shown in Figure 5.5.

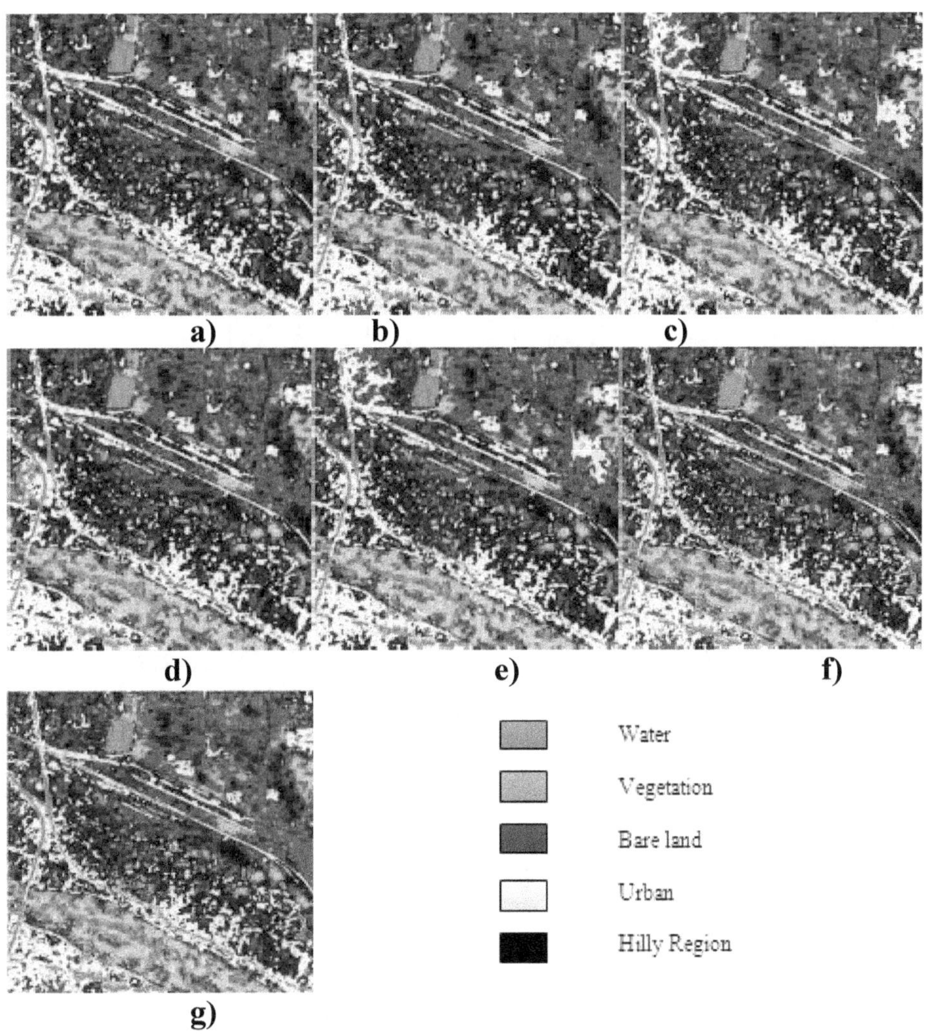


**Figure 5.5 Classified Output using a) Daubechies wavelet b) Coiflet wavelet c) Symlet wavelet d) Bio-orthogonal wavelet e) Meyer wavelet f) GHM Multiwavelet g) CL Multiwavelet**

Results using Different Wavelet and Multiwavelet transform:

Experimental study was carried out for the different scalar and multiwavelet frame based features for classification of LISS IV (ii) Madurai image. The confusion matrices obtained from the classification results using Daubechies wavelet, Coiflet wavelet, Symlet wavelet, bio-orthogonal wavelet Meyer wavelet, GHM & CL multiwavelet methods are shown in Tables 5.1-5.7 respectively.

**Table 5.1 Confusion Matrix using Daubechies Wavelet**

| **LISS IV(ii)** | Urban | Vegetation | Waste land | Hilly | Water | Total row |
|---|---|---|---|---|---|---|
| Urban | 142 | 4 | 5 | 2 | 0 | 153 |
| Vegetation | 3 | 126 | 2 | 6 | 3 | 140 |
| Waste land | 4 | 2 | 121 | 1 | 4 | 132 |
| Hilly | 3 | 5 | 2 | 151 | 5 | 166 |
| Water | 5 | 0 | 3 | 2 | 99 | 109 |
| Total column | 157 | 137 | 133 | 162 | 111 | 700 |

**Table 5.2 Confusion Matrix using Coiflet Wavelet**

| **LISS IV(ii)** | Urban | Vegetation | Waste land | Hilly | Water | Total row |
|---|---|---|---|---|---|---|
| Urban | 139 | 7 | 9 | 8 | 1 | 164 |
| Vegetation | 2 | 125 | 3 | 8 | 0 | 138 |
| Waste land | 4 | 0 | 119 | 1 | 2 | 126 |
| Hilly | 4 | 3 | 2 | 149 | 8 | 166 |
| Water | 5 | 0 | 2 | 1 | 98 | 106 |
| Total column | 154 | 135 | 135 | 167 | 109 | 700 |

**Table 5.3 Confusion Matrix using Symlet Wavelet**

| **LISS IV(ii)** | Urban | Vegetation | Waste land | Hilly | Water | Total row |
|---|---|---|---|---|---|---|
| Urban | 137 | 8 | 12 | 1 | 7 | 165 |
| Vegetation | 4 | 122 | 3 | 5 | 3 | 137 |
| Waste land | 2 | 3 | 117 | 1 | 2 | 125 |
| Hilly | 3 | 3 | 2 | 148 | 8 | 164 |
| Water | 7 | 0 | 4 | 1 | 97 | 109 |
| Total column | 153 | 136 | 138 | 156 | 117 | 700 |

**Table 5.4 Confusion Matrix using Bio-orthogonal Wavelet**

| **LISS IV(ii)** | Urban | Vegetation | Waste land | Hilly | Water | Total row |
|---|---|---|---|---|---|---|
| Urban | 136 | 9 | 7 | 9 | 1 | 162 |
| Vegetation | 4 | 120 | 4 | 8 | 1 | 137 |
| Waste land | 4 | 3 | 115 | 1 | 6 | 129 |
| Hilly | 4 | 3 | 4 | 147 | 8 | 166 |
| Water | 8 | 0 | 2 | 1 | 95 | 106 |
| Total column | 156 | 135 | 132 | 166 | 111 | 700 |

**Table 5.5 Confusion Matrix using Meyer Wavelet**

| **LISS IV(ii)** | Urban | Vegetation | Waste land | Hilly | Water | Total row |
|---|---|---|---|---|---|---|
| Urban | 134 | 8 | 7 | 6 | 2 | 157 |
| Vegetation | 5 | 119 | 8 | 5 | 4 | 141 |
| Waste land | 4 | 3 | 110 | 4 | 6 | 127 |
| Hilly | 3 | 5 | 7 | 144 | 11 | 170 |
| Water | 8 | 0 | 4 | 1 | 92 | 105 |
| Total column | 154 | 135 | 136 | 160 | 115 | 700 |

**Table 5.6 Confusion Matrix using GHM Multiwavelet**

| **LISS IV(ii)** | Urban | Vegetation | Waste land | Hilly | Water | Total row |
|---|---|---|---|---|---|---|
| Urban | 143 | 7 | 8 | 6 | 0 | 164 |
| Vegetation | 4 | 128 | 2 | 1 | 2 | 137 |
| Waste land | 2 | 4 | 122 | 0 | 1 | 129 |
| Hilly | 3 | 0 | 2 | 152 | 4 | 161 |
| Water | 4 | 0 | 3 | 1 | 101 | 109 |
| Total column | 156 | 139 | 137 | 160 | 108 | 700 |

**Table 5.7 Confusion Matrix using CL Multiwavelet**

| **LISS IV(ii)** | Urban | Vegetation | Waste land | Hilly | Water | Total row |
|---|---|---|---|---|---|---|
| Urban | 144 | 6 | 5 | 4 | 1 | 160 |
| Vegetation | 3 | 129 | 1 | 6 | 2 | 141 |
| Waste land | 2 | 3 | 124 | 1 | 0 | 130 |
| Hilly | 4 | 0 | 3 | 153 | 3 | 163 |
| Water | 2 | 0 | 2 | 0 | 102 | 106 |
| Total column | 155 | 138 | 135 | 164 | 108 | 700 |

The quantitative results obtained with the classified map, shown in Tables 5.1- 5.7 are summarized in the Table 5.8. By observing Table 5.8, it is evident that CL Multiwavelet wavelet frame based features gave better results.

**Table 5.8 Results for Different Wavelet & Multiwavelet transforms**

| Different Wavelet& Multiwavelet Transforms | Accuracy indices | | | |
|---|---|---|---|---|
| | User Accuracy | Producer Accuracy | Overall Accuracy | Kappa |
| Daubechies wavelet | 86.1 | 84.4 | 88.3 | 0.8964 |
| Coiflet wavelet | 85.5 | 83.2 | 87.6 | 0.8871 |
| Symlet wavelet | 84.35 | 82.78 | 86.0 | 0.8746 |
| Bio-orthogonal wavelet | 83.8 | 81.8 | 85.4 | 0.8546 |
| Meyer wavelet | 82.2 | 80.6 | 84.2 | 0.8444 |
| GHM Multiwavelet | 87.27 | 85.0 | 89.60 | 0.9024 |
| CL Multiwavelet | 88.2 | 86.6 | 90.9 | 0.919 |

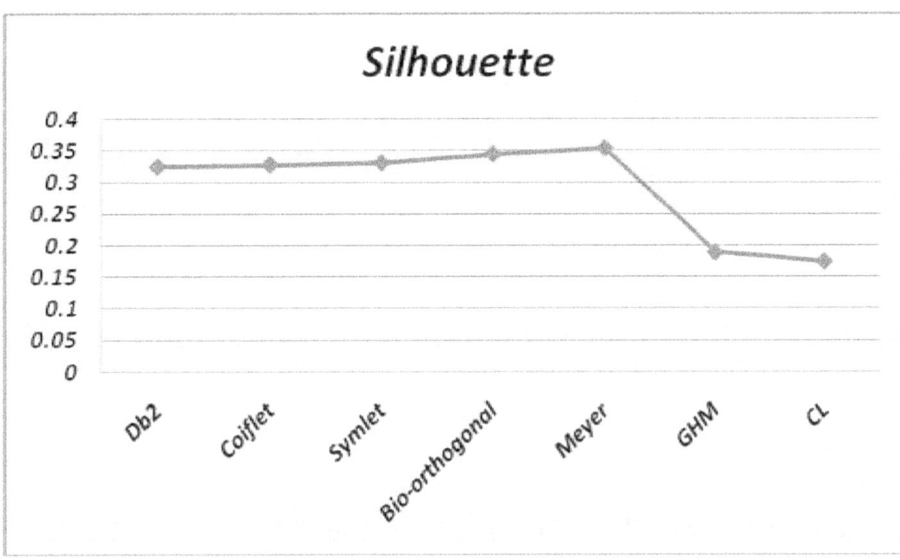


**Figure 5.6 Cluster Validity index using Silhoutte value**

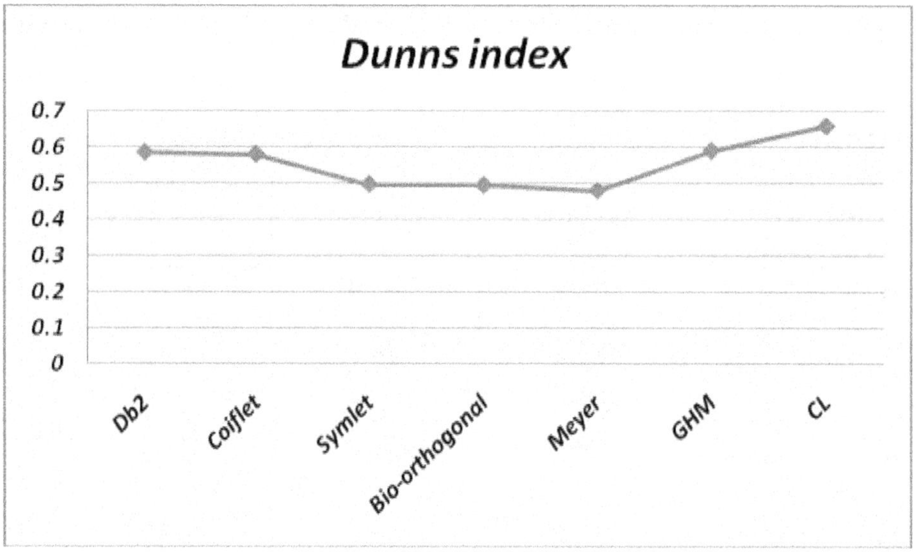


**Figure 5.7 Cluster Validity index using Dunns index**

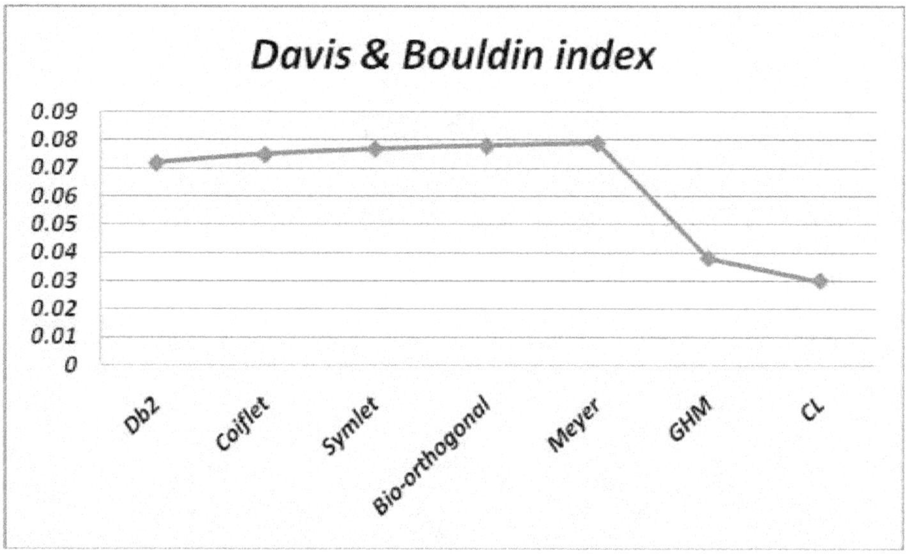


**Figure 5.8 Cluster Validity measures using Davis and Bouldin index**

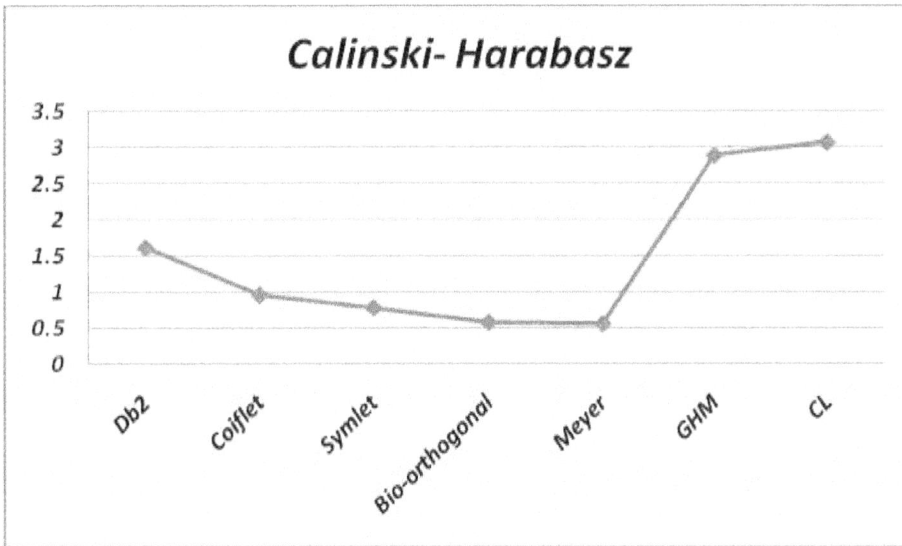


**Figure 5.9 Cluster Validity measures using Calinski Harabasz**

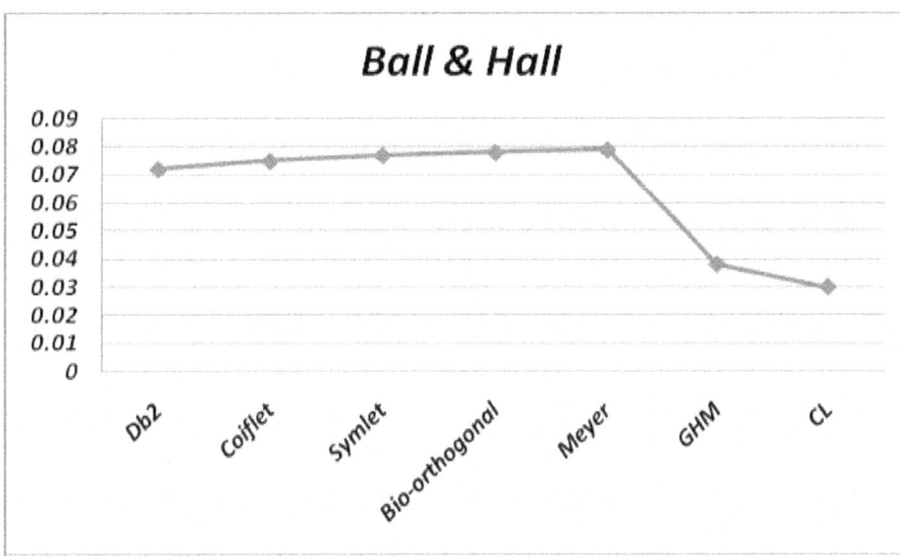


**Figure 5.10 Cluster Validity index using Ball and Hall**

It is evident from the graph 5.6- 5.10, the cluster validity measures for classified LISS IV(ii) image shows CL based Multiwavelet frame transform provides better cluster validity results.

# CHAPTER 6
# LAND USE /LAND COVER MAPPING USING MULTICONTOURLET FRAME BASED FEATURES

This Chapter details the combination of Chui-Lian multiwavelet and Non subsampled contourlet frame based features for improving classification accuracy of satellite images. The performance analysis of CL multicontourlet was compared with wavelet based contourlet transform using LISS II, LISS III, LISS IV(i) images and Chui-Lian multiwavelet using LISS IV(ii) image.

## 6.1 MULTICONTOURLET FRAME BASED FEATURE EXTRACTION

Multicontourlet is a flexible multiscale, multiresolution and multidirectional image decomposition method that provides better direction selectivity and energy convergence compared to that of a multiwavelet. The multicontourlet transform is suitable for representing the remote sensing images bearing abundant detailed (Xia chang et al 2010) and directional information. It is used to capture the higher geometrical content in remote sensing images. Multicontourlet transform maintains the excellent characteristics of multiwavelet transform and removes the anisotropic redundancy in satellite images. The different stages to obtain the multicontourlet frame based features are given below.

**Stage 1**: Pre filter the input images

**Stage 2**: Apply Multiwavelet frame transform (MWFT) to the input images to effectively capture the point discontinuity

**Stage 3**: Apply Non subsampled directional filter banks to the high frequency subbands of each multiwavelet frame decomposition for high directional selectivity.

**Stage 4:**Form the feature vector and perform feature reduction using principal component analysis

**Stage 5:** Apply Gaussian Kernel Fuzzy classifier to classify the features

**Stage 6:** Perform accuracy assessment using ground truth data and cluster validity measures

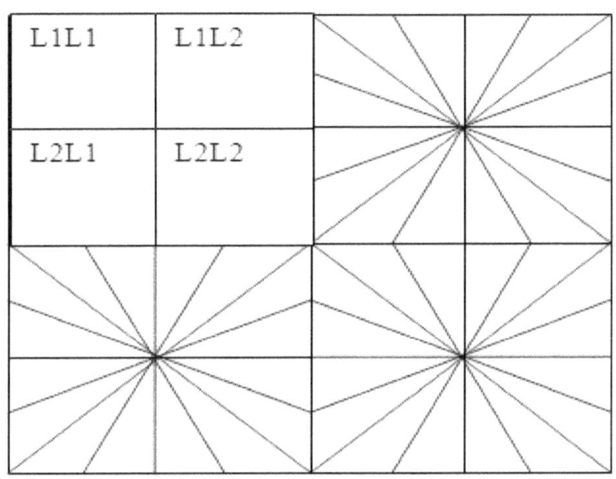


**Figure 6.1 Single level decomposition of Multicontourlet transform**

Single level decomposition of Multicontourlet transform shown in Figure 6.1 is constructed using two parts viz., multiwavelet decomposition and NSDFB decomposition. Firstly the multiwavelet transform was applied to produce approximation and detailed subbands. The NSDFB allowed the direction decomposition with F stages in detailed subbands from SWT at each scale resulting in $2^r$ directional subbands with the same size as the source image.

(Do & Vetterli 2005) proposed a new directional filter banks based on the quincunx filter banks and the fan filters. Such directional filter decomposition does not require modulating the input images. Tree expansion rule is easy to be implemented in the filter banks. The wedge-shaped directional subbands with number $2^l$ were obtained after DFB $l$-level binary tree decomposition. The frequency partition of DFB was realized via appropriate combination of quincunx filter banks and "rotation" operations. The quincunx sampling matrices of DFB are

$$Q_0 = \begin{pmatrix} 1 & -1 \\ 1 & 1 \end{pmatrix} \qquad Q_1 = \begin{pmatrix} 1 & 1 \\ -1 & 1 \end{pmatrix} \tag{6.1}$$

After the first two level of filtering, four directional high-frequency sub bands was obtained. In order to achieve the better frequency division, quincunx filter banks and resamplers are used from the third level. Resampling operation was done by four basic unimodular matrices has a function of rotation the direction of sub bands. The unimodular matrices are denoted as

$$R_0 = \begin{pmatrix} 1 & 1 \\ 0 & 1 \end{pmatrix} \quad R_1 = \begin{pmatrix} 1 & -1 \\ 0 & 1 \end{pmatrix} \quad R_2 = \begin{pmatrix} 1 & 0 \\ 1 & 1 \end{pmatrix} \quad R_3 = \begin{pmatrix} 1 & 0 \\ -1 & 1 \end{pmatrix} \tag{6.2}$$

$R_0$ and $R_1$ are employed in the first half of the DFB channels in order to produce high-frequency subbands in the directions between +45° and −45°; $R2$ and $R3$ are employed in the second half of the channels to produce high-frequency subbands corresponding to the remaining directions from the third level.

With the output from Multiwavelet transform, the non subsampled directional filter banks are applied to extract the detail components from the multiwavelet features. As the output of the one level decomposition of multiwavelet transform has 16 sub bands, NSDFB was applied to 12 high frequency subbands leaving the 4 approximation coefficients. By applying directional filter banks of $2^4$(l=4) to the detail components it provides 196 features and by including the 4 approximation coefficients. Compared to scalar wavelets multiwavelets gave more number of detail components. The process was repeated up to maximum level of decomposition. Thus the accuracy of the image was still improved compared to Multiwavelet frame transform.

## 6.2 EXPERIMENTAL RESULTS AND DISCUSSIONS

The Classified image of LISS IV (ii) using multicontourlet transform is shown in Figure 6.2. Experimental study was carried out to select the best feature extraction method for the classification of LISS IV (ii) Madurai image using multicontourlet transform. The confusion matrices obtained from the classification results using multicontourlet transform are shown in Table 6.1 respectively.

Results using LISS IV (ii) image

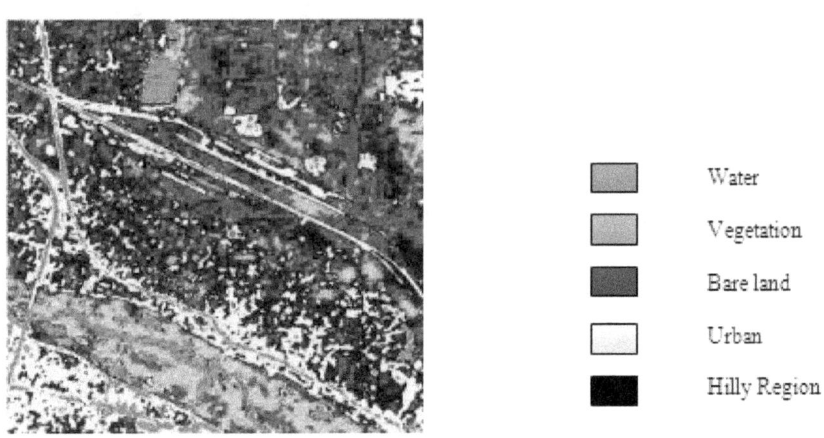


**Figure 6.2 Classified Multicontourlet output for LISS IV(ii) image**

**Table 6.1 Confusion Matrix using Multicontourlet transform for LISS IV(ii) image**

| **LISS IV(ii)** | Urban | Vegetation | Waste land | Hilly | Water | Total row |
|---|---|---|---|---|---|---|
| Urban | 145 | 4 | 5 | 3 | 0 | 157 |
| Vegetation | 2 | 131 | 0 | 4 | 2 | 139 |
| Waste land | 1 | 3 | 125 | 3 | 0 | 132 |
| Hilly | 3 | 0 | 1 | 155 | 4 | 163 |
| Water | 2 | 0 | 2 | 1 | 104 | 109 |
| Total column | 153 | 138 | 133 | 166 | 110 | 700 |

**Table 6.2 Results for LISS IV (ii) image for CL based Multiwavelet and Multicontourlet transform**

| **LISS IV(ii) image** | **Accuracy indices** | | | |
|---|---|---|---|---|
| | User Accuracy | Producer Accuracy | Overall Accuracy | Kappa |
| CL Multiwavelet | 88.2 | 86.6 | 90.9 | 0.919 |
| Multicontourlet | 90.17 | 89.83 | 92.88 | 0.9244 |

By observing the Table 6.2, it is evident that multicontourlet transform gives better results for LISS IV (ii) image..

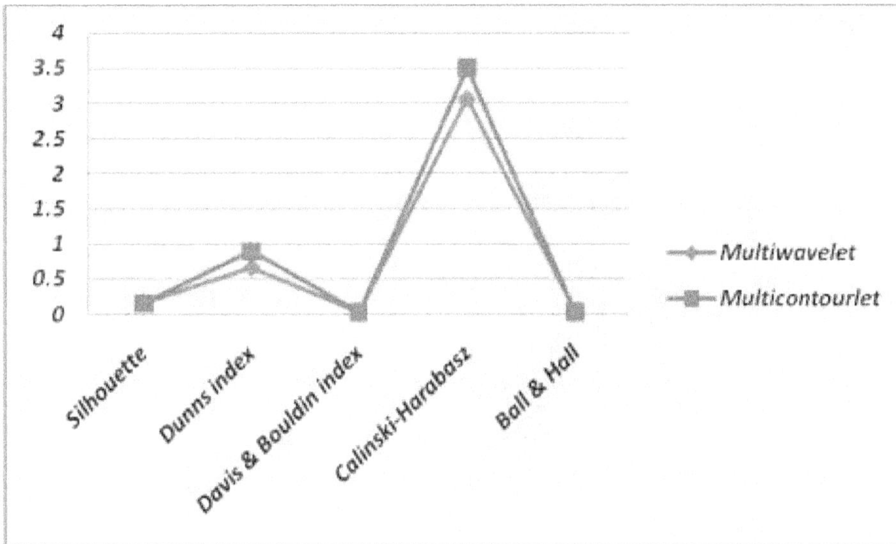


**Figure 6.3 Comparision between Multiwavelet and Multicontourlet transform**

It was evident from the Figure 6.3, for LISS IV (ii) images compared to Multiwavelet frame based features, multicontourlet frame based features gave better cluster validity results.

The Classified images of LISS II, LISS III, LISS IV (i) using multicontourlet transform is shown in Figure. 6.4- 6.6. Experimental study was carried out to select the best feature extraction method for the classification of LISS II, LISS III and LISS IV (i) Madurai images using multicontourlet transform. The confusion matrices obtained from the classification results using multicontourlet transforms are shown in Tables 6.3- 6.5 respectively.

Results using LISS II image

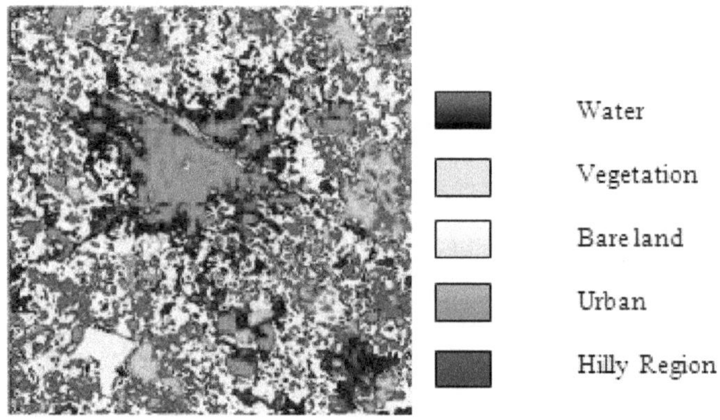


**Figure 6.4 Classified Multicontourlet output for LISS II image**

**Table 6.3 Confusion Matrix using Multicontourlet transform for LISS II image**

| **LISS II** | Urban | Vegetation | Waste land | Hilly | Water | Total row |
|---|---|---|---|---|---|---|
| Urban | 145 | 8 | 8 | 9 | 5 | 175 |
| Vegetation | 9 | 140 | 4 | 4 | 3 | 160 |
| Waste land | 3 | 3 | 126 | 5 | 5 | 142 |
| Hilly | 1 | 1 | 2 | 94 | 3 | 101 |
| Water | 4 | 3 | 3 | 3 | 109 | 122 |
| Total column | 162 | 155 | 143 | 115 | 125 | 700 |

Results using LISS III image

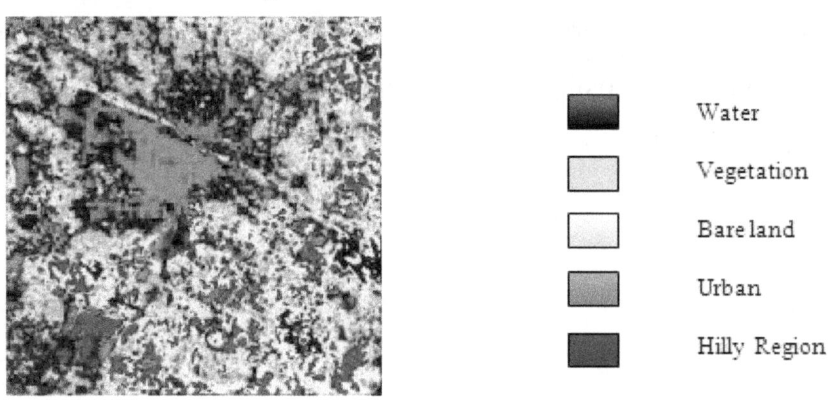


**Figure 6.5 Classified Multicontourlet output for LISS III image**

**Table 6.4 Confusion Matrix using Multicontourlet transform for LISS III image**

| **LISS III** | Urban | Vegetation | Waste land | Hilly | Water | Total row |
|---|---|---|---|---|---|---|
| Urban | 146 | 8 | 7 | 9 | 5 | 175 |
| Vegetation | 8 | 141 | 4 | 4 | 3 | 160 |
| Waste land | 3 | 3 | 128 | 4 | 4 | 142 |
| Hilly | 1 | 1 | 1 | 95 | 3 | 101 |
| Water | 3 | 3 | 3 | 3 | 110 | 122 |
| Total column | 161 | 156 | 143 | 115 | 125 | 700 |

Results using LISS IV(i)image

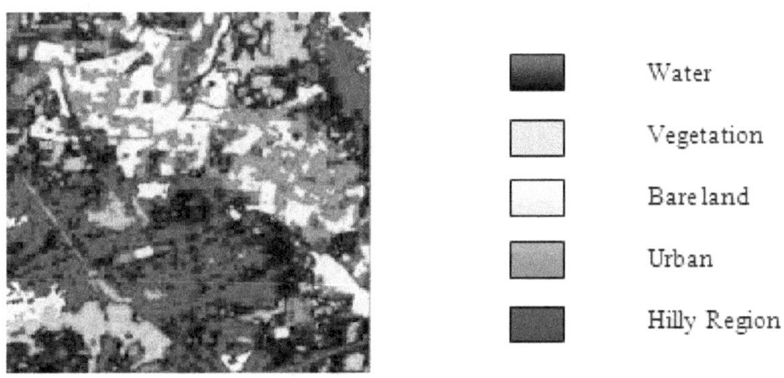


**Figure 6.6 Classified Multicontourlet output for LISS IV(i) image**

**Table 6.5 Confusion Matrix using Multicontourlet transform for LISS IV (i) image**

| **LISS IV(i)** | Urban | Vegetation | Waste land | Hilly | Water | Total row |
|---|---|---|---|---|---|---|
| Urban | 148 | 7 | 7 | 8 | 5 | 175 |
| Vegetation | 6 | 143 | 4 | 4 | 3 | 160 |
| Waste land | 3 | 3 | 129 | 3 | 4 | 142 |
| Hilly | 1 | 1 | 1 | 97 | 1 | 101 |
| Water | 2 | 2 | 3 | 3 | 112 | 122 |
| Total column | 160 | 156 | 144 | 115 | 125 | 700 |

**Table 6.6 Results for LISS II LISS III and LISS IV (i) image for Multicontourlettransform**

| LISS image | Accuracy indices | | | |
|---|---|---|---|---|
| | User Accuracy | Producer Accuracy | Overall Accuracy | Kappa |
| LISS II | 84.0 | 81.2 | 87.3 | 0.888 |
| LISS III | 85.6 | 84.2 | 88.3 | 0.902 |
| LISS IV(i) | 90.1 | 88.7 | 92.5 | 0.934 |

The quantitative results obtained with the classified map, shown in Tables 6.3- 6.5 are summarized in the Table 6.6. By observing Table 6.6, it is evident that multicontourlet frame transform gave better results than wavelet based contourlet transform for LISS II,LISS III,LISS IV (i) images.

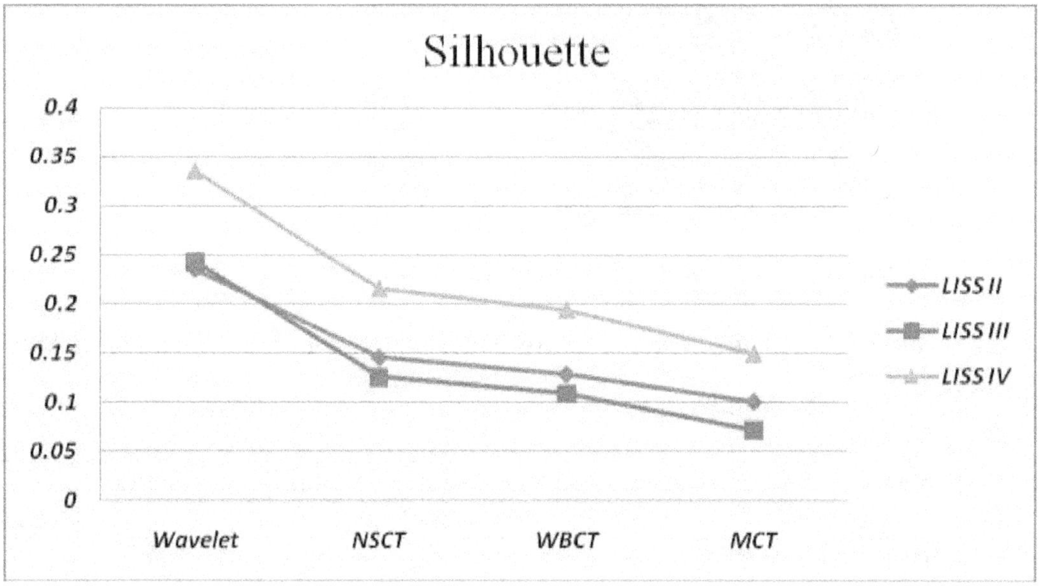


**Figure 6.7 Cluster Validity measures Using Silhouette Value**

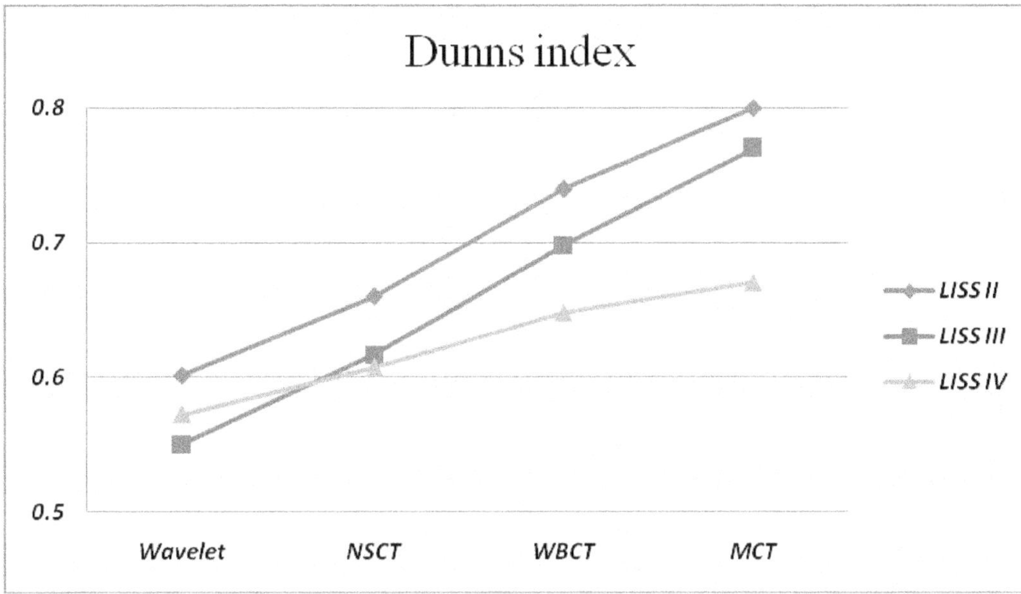


**Figure 6.8 Cluster Validity measures Using DB index**

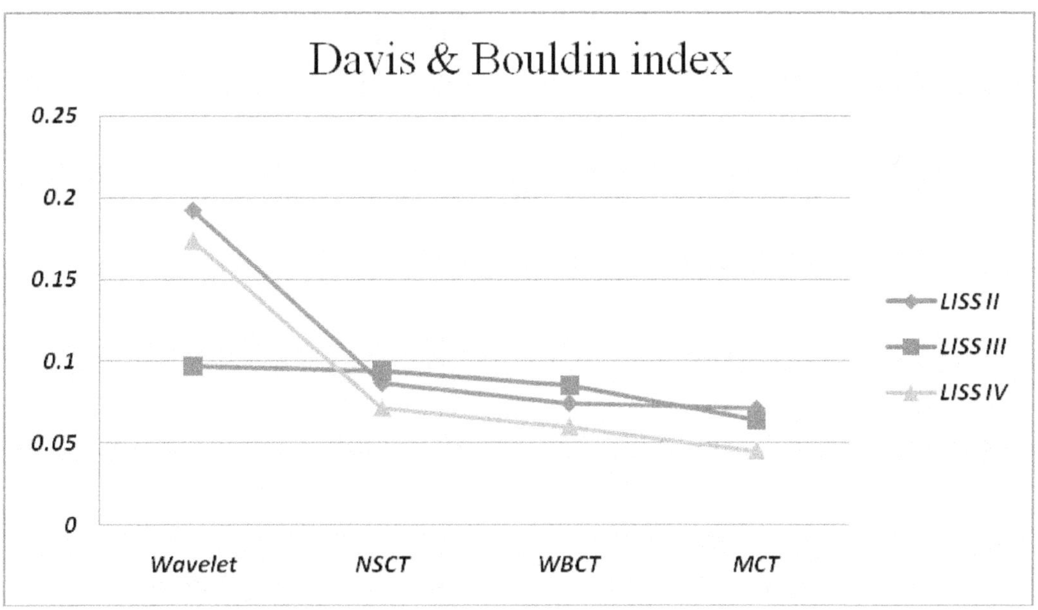


**Figure 6.9 Cluster Validity measures using Davis Bouldin index**

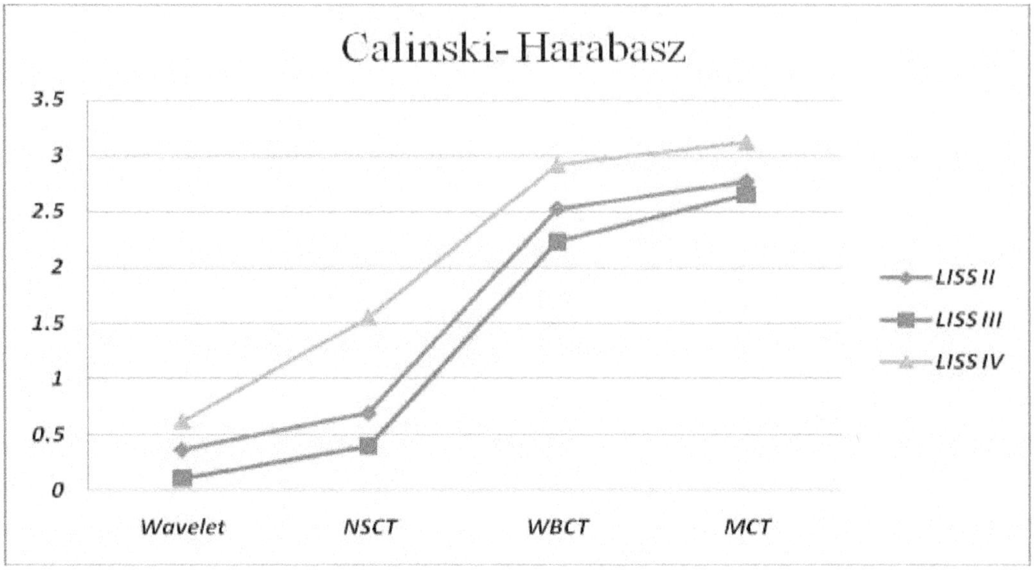


**Figure 6.10 Cluster Validity measures using Calinski -Harabasz**

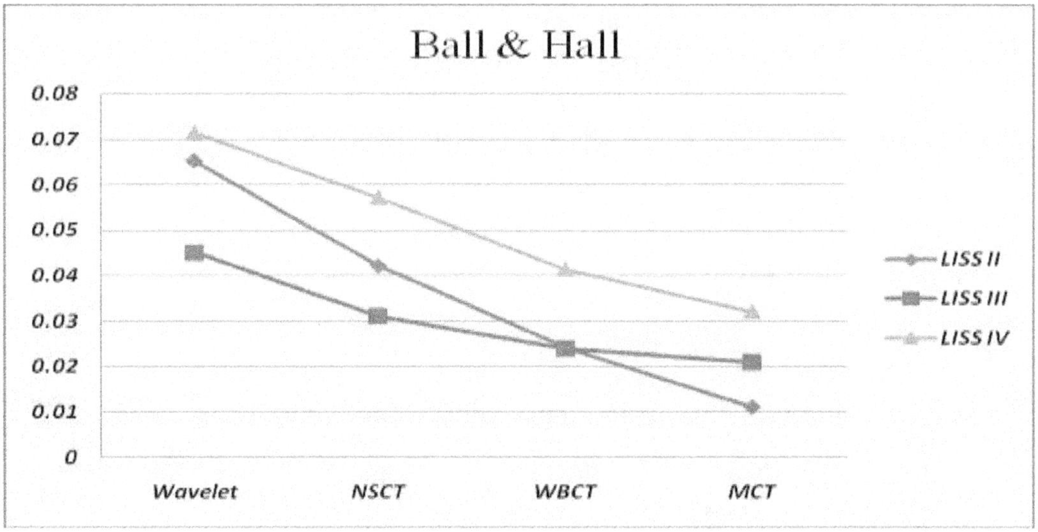


**Figure 6.11 Cluster Validity measures using Ball and Hall**

It is evident from the graph shown in Figure 6.7-6.11 the cluster validity measures for LISS II, LISS III and LISS IV(i) images gave better validity results for multicontourlet frame based features compared to wavelet ,NSCT ,WBCT frame transform.

# CHAPTER 7

# DISCUSSION OVER THE PROPOSED METHODS

This chapter discusses the performance of the proposed methods in chapter IV, Chapter V and Chapter VI

## 7.1 DISCUSSION

To demonstrate the effectiveness of the proposed approach different contourlet frame based texture feature extraction techniques were implemented in chapter IV. The performance analyses of these techniques were carried out using the ground truth data and the cluster validity measures. In the existing method of wavelet frame based feature extraction, due to the lack of the directional components results in less accuracy. Non subsampled contourlet transform extracts the detailed components of the high frequency images. Compared to the wavelet frame transform (LISS – II kappa 0.8144, LISS – III kappa 0.844 and LISS – IV(i) kappa 0.846) Non subsampled contourlet frame transform (LISS – II kappa 0.8368, LISS – III kappa 0.854 and LISS – IV (i) kappa 0.865) gave better accuracy results. Wavelet analyzes the features at multiple resolutions. Many features have dominant frequency in high and middle frequency images. Contourlet focussing on the dominant frequency region gave more spatial frequency information. Wavelet based contourlet transform gave more spatial frequency information and at the same time additionally it extracted the spatial frequency information from directional subbands. Compared to the existing and proposed techniques discussed in this chapter IV, scalar wavelet based contourlet frame transform gave unique spatial frequency signatures that resulted in higher (LISS – II kappa 0.8785, LISS – III kappa 0.871 and LISS – IV(i) kappa 0.894) accuracy and better cluster validity measures.

Multiwavelet an extension to scalar wavelets provides higher degree of freedom, which possess two or more scaling function and wavelet function. The performance analysis of the scalar and multiwavelets were carried out using the ground truth data and the cluster validity measures in chapter V. Scalar wavelet frame based features leads to less accuracy compared to multiwavelets. Daubechies wavelets (LISS – IV (ii) kappa 0.8964) and Bio orthogonal wavelets (LISS – IV (ii) kappa 0.8546) are compactly supported wavelets with extremely phase and highest number of vanishing moments for a given support width. Symlet wavelets (LISS – IV **(ii)** kappa 0.8746) are compactly supported wavelets with least asymmetry and highest number of vanishing moments for a given support width. Meyer (LISS – IV (ii) kappa 0.8444) & Coiflet (LISS – IV (ii) kappa 0.8871) wavelets are compactly supported wavelets with the highest number of vanishing moments for phi and psi for a given support width. Multiwavelet satisfies several mathematical properties simultaneously such as orthogonality, compact support, linear phase symmetry and higher order approximation. Many features have dominant frequency in high and middle frequency images. Multiwavelet transform provided higher number of subbands focusing on the approximation coefficient gives more detail spatial frequency information. Compared to the scalar and GHM (LISS – IV (ii) kappa 0.9024), CL multiwavelet techniques discussed in this Chapter V Multiwavelet frame transform gave unique spatial frequency signatures that leads to higher (LISS – IV (ii) kappa 0.919) accuracy and better cluster validity results.

Multicontourlet is a flexible multi scale, multi resolution and multidirectional image decomposition method that provided better direction selectivity and energy convergence compared to that of multiwavelets. The performance comparison of the multicontourlet transform was carried out using the ground truth data and cluster validity measures. In the existing method scalar wavelet and contourlet frame based feature extraction is implemented, due to the less number of features extracted it leads to less accuracy (LISS – II kappa 0.8785, LISS – III kappa 0.871 and LISS – IV(i) kappa 0.894). Compared to scalar wavelets, Multiwavelets possess properties such as compact support, symmetry, short support and vanishing moments. Multiwavelet analyzes the features at multiple resolutions with linear phase symmetry and higher order approximation (LISS IV (ii) kappa 0.919). Nonsubsampled contourlet frame focusing on the dominant frequency region gave more spatial frequency information. Multicontourlet transform represents the images with abundant detail and directional information and it leads to higher accuracy (LISS – II kappa 0.888, LISS – III kappa 0.902, LISS – IV(i) kappa 0.934), LISS IV(ii) kappa0.9244) and better cluster validity results. Compared to the existing and proposed techniques discussed in this research work, Multicontourlet frame based features gave better accuracy results for classification in satellite images.

# CHAPTER 8

# CONCLUSION AND FUTURE ENHANCEMENT

This Chapter gives the conclusion with a summary of the outcomes of the research work and future research issues that needs to be addressed.

## 8.1 THESIS CONTRIBUTION

This thesis has presented a systematic approach for the classification of satellite images using different multiscale and multidirection transform based texture feature extraction techniques.

The following conclusions are drawn from the work presented in the thesis i)In Chapter 4 the performance of the wavelet, Non subsampled contourlet, Wavelet based contourlet frame based features for the classification of satellite images using LISS II,LISS III,LISS IV (i) madurai imagery is discussed. The scalar wavelet and contourlet frame based texture features were found to be effective for the classification of satellite images ii) In chapter 5. The performance analysis of the different scalar wavelets was compared with multiwavelets using LISS IV (ii) Madurai imagery. Compared to scalar and GHM Multiwavelets CL Multiwavelets gave higher accuracy for the classification of satellite images iii) In chapter 6, the combination of CL Multiwavelet and Non subsampled contourlet frame transform has been tested and the performance was compared with CL Multiwavelet and Wavelet based contourlet frame transform for classification of satellite images. Multicontourlet frame based feature significantly increased the directional features and gave better accuracy results compared to the existing feature extraction methods.

## 8.2 CONCLUSION

To demonstrate the effectiveness of the proposed approach different contourlet frame based feature extraction techniques were implemented. The performance comparisons of these techniques were carried out using the ground truth data and the cluster validity measures. In the existing method wavelet frame based feature extraction, due to the lack of the directional components it resulted in less accuracy. Non subsampled contourlet transform extracted the detailed components of the high frequency images. Compared to the wavelet frame transform (LISS – II kappa 0.9184, LISS – III kappa 0.9042 and LISS – IV(i) kappa 0.908) Non subsampled contourlet transform (LISS – II kappa 0.8144, LISS – III kappa 0.844 and LISS – IV(i) kappa 0.846) gave better accuracy results. Wavelet analyzed the features at multiple resolutions. Many features have dominant frequency in high and middle frequency images. Contourlet focussing on the dominant frequency region gave more spatial frequency information. Wavelet based contourlet transform gave more spatial frequency information and at the same time additionally it extracts the spatial frequency information from directional subbands(LISS – II kappa 0.8785, LISS – III kappa 0.871 and LISS – IV(i) kappa 0.894). Multiwavelet satisfies several mathematical properties simultaneously such as orthogonality, compact support, linear phase symmetry and higher order approximation. Compared to the scalar wavelets Multiwavelets gave better accuracy results. Multicontourlet representing the images with abundant detail and directional information and it resulted in higher accuracy (LISS – II kappa 0.888, LISS – III kappa 0.902 and LISS – IV(i) kappa 0.934). Cluster validity measures also showed that the Multicontourlet frame based features gave better validity results. Compared to the existing and proposed techniques discussed in this research Multicontourlet frame based features gave better results for classification of satellite images.

## 8.3 FUTURE ENHANCEMENT

Scalar Wavelets, Contourlets, Multiwavelets have been used in this research work. Use of other Multiwavelets and complex wavelets with the combination of contourlets were the few areas to be investigated in the future.

PCA has been used for dimensionality reduction. In future, the utilization of other dimensionality reduction methods may also could be studied.

Gaussian kernel fuzzy classifiers are used to improve the classification accuracy. Similarly the use of fuzzy with multiple kernels may also be investigated.

# REFERENCES


1. Abdullah Al Jumah, Mohammed Gulam Ahamad & Syed Amjad Ali 2013, 'Denoising of Medical Images Using Multiwavelet Transforms and Various Thresholding Techniques', Journal of Signal and Information Processing, vol. 4, pp. 24-32.

2. Abu-Zeid, N, Kashif, R & Badawy, OM 2012, 'Immune Based Clustering for Medical Diagnostic Systems', IEEE Xplore Advanced Computer Science Applications and Technologies, pp. 372 – 375.

3. Acharyya, M & Kundu, Mk 2001, „Adaptive Basis Selection For Multi Texture Segmentation By M-Band Wavelet Packet Frames", IEEE Proceedings of the International Conference on Image Processing, vol. 2, pp. 622-625.

4. Acharyya, M & Kundu, Mk 2001a, 'Wavelet-Based Texture Segmentation Of Remotely Sensed Images', IEEE International Conference On Image Analysis And Processing, pp. 69-74.

5. Acharyya, M, Rajat, K, De & Kundu, Mk 2003, „Segmentation Of Remotely Sensed Images Using Wavelet Features And Their Evaluation In Soft Computing Framework", IEEE Transations on Geoscience And Remote Sensing", vol. 41, pp. 2900-2905.

6. Aili Wang & Chunhui Zhao 2012, „SAR Image Feature Extraction and Target Recognition Based on Contourlet and SVM", International Proceedings of Computer Science & Information Tech, vol. 53, no.1, pp. 79.

7. Alagu Raja, RA Anand, V , Maithani, S, Senthil Kumar, A, Abhai Kumar, V 2013, „Wavelet Based Post classification change detection for urban growth monitoring", vol. 44, no. 1, pp. 35-43.

8. Alagu Raja, RA Anand, V, Maithani, S, Senthil Kumar, A & Abhai Kumar, V 2009, „Wavelet frame-based feature extraction technique for improving classification accuracy", Journal of the Indian Society of Remote Sensing, vol. 37, pp. 423-431.

9. Ali Zifan, Mohammad Hassan Moradi & Shahriar Gharibzadeh 2010, 'Microarray Image Enhancement By Denoising Using Decimated And

Undecimated Multiwavelet Transforms', Signal Image And Video Processing, vol. 4, no. 2, pp. 177-185.

10. Amitabh, Gopalakrishna, B, Srinivasan, TP, Srivatsava, PK 2008, „An Integrated Approach for Topographical Mapping from Space using CARTOSAT-1 and CARTOSAT-2 imagery", The International Archives of Photogrametry,Remote Sensing and Spatial Information Sciences.vol.XXXVII part B4.

11. An Zhiyong, Li Jinjiang, Zhao Feng & Guo Jie 2014, 'Image Retrieval Based On The Multiwavelets Texture-Spatial Features', Applied Mathematics & Information Sciences, vol. 2, no. 8, pp. 745-750.

12. Arivazhagan, S & Ganesan L 2003, „Texture Classification Using Wavelet Transform, Pattern Recognition Letters", vol. 24, issues. 9–10, pp. 1513-1521.

13. Arivazhagan, S, Ganeshan, L & Padmam priyal, S 2006, „Texture Classification using Gabor Wavelet Based Rotation Invariant Features", vol. 27, no. 16, pp. 1976-1982.

14. Borges, Js, Marçal, Ars & Dias, Jmb 2007, „Evaluation Of Feature Extraction And Reduction Methods For Hyperspectral Images", New Developments And Challenges In Remote Sensing Ed. Z. Bochenek, pp. 265-274.

15. Cetin, M, Kavzoglu, T & Musaoglu, N 2004, „Classification Of Multispectral, Multi Temporal, Multi Sensor Images Using Principal Component Analysis And Artificial Neural Networks: Beykoz Case" Proceedings International Society For Photgrammetry And Remote Sensing- Xxxv-Congress.

16. Collins, R, Lipton, A & Kanade, T 2000, „Introduction To Special Section On Video Surveillance", IEEE Trans. Pattern Analytics And Machine Intelligence, vol. 22, no. 8, pp. 745-746.

17. Dinesh, Ms, Chidananda Gowda, K & Nagapushban, P 1998, „Analysis Of IRS 1B LISS-II Image Using Fuzzy And Symbolic Approach", IEEE Geoscience And Remote Sensing Proceedings, vol. 2, pp. 779-781.

18. Do, MN & Vetterli, M 2005, „The contourlet transform: an efficient directional multiresolution image representation", IEEE Transactions Image on Processing, vol. 14, no. 12, pp. 2091-2106

19. Do,MN & Vetterli, M 2001, „Pyramidal directional filter banks and Curvelets",Proceedings of the IEEE international conference on Image Processing, Thessaloniki, Greece, pp. 158-161

20. Dumontier, C, Luthon, F & Charras, JP 1999, „Real-time DSP implementation for MRF-based video motion detection,".IEEE.Trans. Image Process", vol. 8, no. 10, pp. 1341–1347.

21. Dwivedi, RS, Ramana, KV, Thammapa KS & Singh, AN 2001, „The Utility of IRS-1C LISS-III and PAN-Merged Data for Mapping Salt-Affected Soils", Photogrammetric Engineering and Remote Sensing, vol. 67, no. 10, pp. 1167-1175.

22. Fanax femy, F & Victor SP 2014, „Feature Extraction using Contourlet transform for glaucomatous Image Classification", vol. 95, no. 18, pp. 20-24.

23. Fauvel, M, Channussot, J, Benediktsson, JA 2006, „Kernel Principal Component Analysis for feature reduction in Hyper spectral Image Analysis", IEEE proceedings of the 7th Nordic signal processing symposium, pp. 238-241.

24. Giles Foody, M 2001, „Status of land cover classification accuracy assessment", Remote Sensing and Environment Elsevier, vol. 80, pp. 185-201.

25. Hamid Soltanian-zadeh, Farshid Rafiee-rad & Siamak Pourabdollah-nejad D 2004, „Comparison of multiwavelet, wavelet, Haralick and shape features for microcalcification classification in mammograms", Journal of Pattern Recognition - PR , vol. 37, no. 10, pp. 1973-1986.

26. Haralick, M 1979, „Statistical and structural approaches to texture", Proceedings of the IEEE, vol.67, no. 5, pp.786-804.

27. Hebbar, R & Sesha sai, MVR 2014, „Comparision of LISS-IV MX and LISS-III+LISS-IV Merged Data for Classification of Crops",ISPRS Technical Symposium VIII Commision, vol. II-8, pp. 101-105.

28. Hizir Sofyan, Md, Azlin Md Said, Muzailin Affan & Khaled Bawahidi 2005, „The Application Of Fuzzy Clustering To Satellite Images Data", Wseas International Conference On Remote Sensing, pp. 117-120.

29. Hoseini, F, Darvishsefat, AA 2012, „Investigating the Capability of IRS-P6-LISS IV Satellite Image for Pistachio Forests Density Mapping" International Archives of the Photogrammetry, Remote Sensing and Spatial Information Sciences, vol. XXXIX-B8, pp. 409-411.

30. Hsu-Shen Tsai,Wen Lian Hung, Min & Shen Yang 2012, „A robust kernel-based fuzzy c-means algorithm by incorporating suppressed and magnified membership for MRI image segmentation", Lecture Notes in Computer Science, vol. 7530, pp. 744-754.

31. Ivan, W & Selesnick 1998, 'Multiwavelet Bases with Extra Approximation Properties', IEEE Transactions on Signal Processing, vol. 46, no. 11.

32. Javed, A, Sayema, J & Mohd, YK 2012, „Climate Change Induced Land Degradation and Socio –Economic deterioration.A Remote sensing and GIS based Case study from Rajasthan,India", Journal of Geographic Information System, vol. 4, pp. 219-228.

33. Jayantha Kumar Ghosh, Pramod Narayan God Bole & Sanjay Kumar Ghosh, „A fuzzy knowledge based interpreting system is applied on the geocoded images for the mapping of tea gardens in the cacher district in assam india imagery", The International Archives of Photogrametry,Remote Sensing, vol. XXXIII part.B7.

34. Kaliraj, S & Chandrasekar, N 2012, „Spectral Recognition Techniques and MLC of IRS P6 LISS III image for Coastal Landforms Extraction along South West Coast of Tamil Nadu, India", Bonfring International Journal on Advances in Image Processing,vol. 2 ,no. 3, pp. 1-7.

35. Kavita, Anandrao, Khobragade & Kale, KV 2014, 'Multi-Wavelet Based Feature Extraction Algorithm For Iris Recognition', International Journal of Engineering And Innovative Technology, Ijeit, vol. 3, no. 12, pp. 368-373.

36. Kavitha, K, Arivazhagan, S & Kayalvizhi, N 2010, „Wavelet Based Spatial - Spectral Hyperspectral Image Classification Technique Using Support Vector Machines", IEEE International conference on Computing and Communication and Networking Technologies, pp. 1-6.

37. Kimothi, MM, Anitha, D, Vasistha, HB, Soni, P & Chandola, SK 2010, „Remote Sensing to map invasive weed,Lantana camera in forests", Tropical Ecology, vol. 51, no. 1, pp. 67-74.

38. Kiran, Vss, Srivastava, Yk & Jagannadha Roa, Mk 2014, „Utilization Of Resourcesat LISS IV Data For Infrastructure updation and Land Use/Land Cover Mapping-A Case Study From Simlipal Block, Bankura District, West Bengal‟, International Journal Of Advanced Remote Sensing And GIS, vol. 3, issue.1, pp. 592-597.

39. Kitti Koonsanit, Chuleerat Jaruskulchai & Apisit Eiumnoh 2012, „Band Selection for Dimension Reduction in Hyper Spectral Image Using Integrated Information Gain and Principal Components Analysis Technique‟, International Journal of Machine Learning and Computing, vol. 2, no. 3, pp. 248-251.

40. Kshama Gupta & Shadana Jain 2005, „Enhanced Capabilities Of IRSp6 LISS IV For Urban Mapping‟, Current Science, vol. 89, no. 11, pp. 1805-1812.

41. Lizarazo, I & Barros, J 2011, „Fuzzy Image Segmentation For Urban Land-Cover Classification „Available From:< Http://Www.Isprs.Org/Proceedings/Xxxviii/4-C1/Sess>

42. Mahmoudi-Barmas, Sh & Kasaei , Sh 2008, „Contourlet-Based Edge Extraction For Image Registration‟, Iranian Journal Of Electrical And Electronic Engineering, vol. 4, no. 1, pp. 17-34.

43. Maria Halkidi, Yannis Batistakis & Michalis Vazirgiannis 2002, „Clustering Validity Checking Methods: Part II‟, ACM SIGMOD Record, vol. 31, no. 3, pp. 19.

44. Maria Halkidi, Yannis Batistakis & Michalis Vazirgiannis 2002a, „Cluster validity Methods: Part-I‟. ACM SIGMOD Record, vol. 31, no. 2„ pp. 40-45.

45. Mattia crespi & Laura De Vendictis 2009, ‟A procedure for High Resolution Satellite Imagery Quality Assessment‟Sensors,vol. 9, pp. 3289-3313.

46. Meher, Sk, Shankar, Bu & Ghosh, A 2007, „Wavelet-Feature-Based Classifiers For Multispectral Remote-Sensing Images‟, IEEE Transactions On Geo Science And Remote Sensing, vol. 45, no. 6, pp. 1881-1886.

47. Negi, HS, Thakur, NK, Ganju, A & Snehmani 2012, „Monitoring of Gangotri glacier using remote sensing and ground observations“, Journal of Earth System Sciences, vol. 121.no. 4.pp. 855-866.

48. Petcu, D, Zaharie, D, Panica, S, Huessein, AS, Sayed, A & Shishiney, HE 2011, „Fuzzy clustering of large satellite images using high performance computing“, SPIE Proceedings of International Conference on High-Performance Computing in Remote Sensing,ed. Borming Huang, Antonia J. Plaza 818302.

49. Pooneh Bagheri Zadeh & Cristian, V, Serdean 2011, 'Multiwavelets in the Context Of Hierarchical Stereo Correspondence Matching Techniques', International Journal On Advances In Telecommunications, vol. 4, no. 1 & 2.

50. Radhadevi, PV Solanki, SS, Jyothi, MV, Nagasubramaniam, V & Geeta. V 2009, „Automated Co-Registration of Images from Multiple Bands of LISS-IV Camera“ ISPRS Journal of Photogrammetry and Remote Sensing, vol. 64. no. 1, pp. 17-26.

51. Raghu Babu, KR 2012, „Spectral analysis of IRS P6 LISS III image for gold associated minerals in veligallu schisttarea, Kadapa district, Andhra pradesh“ International Journal of Advances in Remote Sensing and GIS, vol. 1, no. 1, pp. 18-24.

52. Rajesh, S, Arivazhagan, S, Pratheep Moses, K & Abisekaraj, R 2012, „Land cover/Land use Mapping using different Wavelet Packet transforms for LISS IV Madurai imagery“, vol. 40, no. 2, pp.313-324.

53. Raju, G 2013, „Engineering challenges in the Megha-Tropiques satellite“, Current Science, vol. 104, no. 12, pp. 1662-1670.

54. Ramakrishnan, S & Selven, S 2007, 'Multiwavelets Domain Singular Value Features For Image Texture Classification', Journal Of Zhejiang University Science A, vol. 8, no. 4, pp. 538-549.

55. Randen, T, Schlumberger Geco-Prakla, Stavanger, Norway & Husoy, Jh 1999, „Filtering For Texture Classification: A Comparative Study“, Pattern Analysis And Machine, vol. 21, no. 4.

56. Rejaur Rahman, MD, Hedayutul Islam, AHM, Ataur Rahman, MD, „Normalized difference vegetation index derived sugarcane area identification and crop condition assessment ,<.Available from

http://www.ida.liu.se/~746A27/Literature/NDVI%20derived%20sugar%20cane%20area%20identification.pdf>.

57. Robert M. Haralick, Shanmugam. K & Dinstein, ITSHAK 1973, „Textural Features for image classification", IEEE transactions on systems man and cybernetics, vol. 6, pp. 610-621

58. Sai, T, Lin EK, F & Yoshino, K 2007, „Spectrally segmented principal component analysis of hyperspectral imagery for mapping invasive plant species", vol. 28, no. 5

59. Sasikala, G, Kowsalya, R, Punithavalli, R 2010, „Comparative study of dimensionality reduction techniques using PCA and LDA for content based image retrieval"International Journal of Multimedia and its applications, vol. 2, no. 3, pp. 40-47.

60. Shutai Li & Leyuan Fang & Haitao Yin, „Multitemporal Image Change Detection Using a Detail-Enhancing Approach With Non subsampled Contourlet Transform", IEEE Geoscience and Remote Sensing Letters, vol. 9, no. 5, pp. 836-840.

61. Shutao, LI, Yaonan Wang & Boris Lohmann 2003, 'Texture Classification Using Discrete Multiwavelet Transform', Journal of AMSE B Signal Processing and Pattern Recognition, vol. 46, no. 1-2

62. Singh, M & Singh, S 2002, „Spatial Texture Analysis –A Comparitive Study", 16th International Conference on Pattern Recognition, Proceedings, vol. 1, pp. 676-679.

63. Smriti Bhatnagar & Jain, RC 2015, „A Comparative analysis and applications of Multiwavelet transform in image denoising", International Journal of Cybernetics and Informatics, vol. 4, no. 2.

64. Somasundaram, D & Palaniswami. S 2015, „SFLA Optimization Based Spatial Kernel Fuzzy C-Means Clustering for MRI Image Segmentation using SIFT Descriptors", Australlian Journal of Basic and Applied Sciences, vol. 9, no. 1, pp. 250-257.

65. Soumi Ghosh & Sanjay Kumar Dubey 2013, „A Comparative Analysis of Fuzzy C-Means Clustering and K Means Clustering Algorithms"International Journal of Advanced Computer Science and Applications, vol. 4, no. 4, pp. 35-39.

66. Stamos Katsigiannis,Eystratios, GK & Dimitris Maroulis 2010, „A Contourlet Transform Feature Extraction Scheme for ultrasound Thyroid texture Classification", Artificial Intelligence applications and Innovations, vol. 18, no. 3-4.

67. Supudhi, AP, Badrinath, KVS & Govil, SK 1989, „Digital image processing of IRS LISS II data for urban studies case study of Delhi",.Journal of the Indian Society of Remote Sensing, vol. 17, no. 3, pp. 35-42.

68. Tarik ZI, Aya, AK & Ahkam KN 2013, 'Human Face Recognition using Stationary Multiwavelet Transform', An International Journal of Computer Applications, vol. 72, no. 1, pp. 23-32.

69. Unser Michael & Eden, M 1988, „Multiresolution Feature Extraction and Selection for Texture Segmentation „IEEE Transactions on Pattern Analysis and Machine Intelligence, vol. 11, no. 7, pp. 717-728.

70. Unser, M 1995, „Texture Classification and Segmentation using Wavelet Frames",IEEE Transactions on Image Processing, vol. 4, Issue. 11, pp. 1549-1560

71. Volpi, M, Tuia, D, Camps, VG & Kanevski, M 2012, „Unsupervised Change detection with kernels", EEE Geoscience and Remote Sensing Letters, vol. 9, no. 6, pp. 1026-1030.

72. Weszka, Joan, S, Dyer Charles, R, Rosenfield & Azriel 1976, „Comparative Study of Texture Measures for Terrain Classification", vol.SMC-6, no. 4, pp. 269-285.

73. Xia Chang, Licheng Jiao, Fang Liu & Fangfang Xin 2010, 'Multicontourlet-Based Adaptive Fusion of Infrared and Visible Remote Sensing Images', IEEE Geoscience and Remote Sensing letters, vol. 7, no. 3, pp. 549-553.

74. Zhang, X & Tian, Q 2015, „Comparison Of Spectral Characteristics Between EO-1 ALI And IRS-P6 LISS-III Imagery" vol. 108, no. 5, pp. 954-960.

75. Zhiqiang Zhou & Jingjing Ma 2012, „Change Detection in Synthetic Aperture Radar Images Based on Image Fusion and Fuzzy Clustering", IEEE Transactions on Image Processing, vol. 21, no. 4, pp. 2141-2151

www.ingramcontent.com/pod-product-compliance
Lightning Source LLC
LaVergne TN
LVHW082345200926
848481LV00012B/3453